7708

POSTS-MORTEM

POSTS-MORTEM

The Correspondence of Murder

Jonathan Goodman

David & Charles : Newton Abbot

ISBN o 7153 5389 6

Set in Monotype Plantin
and printed in Great Britain
by Latimer Trend & Company Limited Plymouth
for David & Charles (Publishers) Limited
South Devon House   Newton Abbot   Devon

Contents

Illustrations

Once again for Susan

Introduction

In a vicarious and, of course, law-abiding sense, the crime of murder exerts different fascinations on different people: one man's meat-axe is another man's poison; a particular case, a favourite with one person, may appeal not at all to another, simply because its ingredients, singularly or as a mixture, are not to his criminous taste.

Most murder cases are caviare to the general. There appears to be a single factor common to those rare cases that capture and hold a wide interest, and this is that they are both appropriate to and evocative of the ambience of their period and place. The Ripper crimes of the late 1880s, for instance: one feels that if they had never happened, they would need to have been invented to fill the gap left by their unintended absence, so perfectly do they fit the context of the times, the grim and grimy milieu of the Whitechapel slums. And the Crippen case, which gives a clearer picture of London and Londoners in 1910 than a whole shelf of social history books.

All murder cases (and the *all* is not a thoughtless overstatement) reveal something of their ambience, and this is one of the fascinations of studying them; one of many. There is also the fascination of trying to solve the puzzle inherent in so many of the cases—less often who-did-it than what-made-him-do-it; of watching a great advocate in action, recognising his tricks of rhetoric and presentation, comparing his style in one case with or to his style in another; of seeing a small-part player (the 'pig woman' in the Hall-Mills case is a prime example) suddenly become the star, the headline maker.

A lot of my own homicidal fascinations are on the outskirts of cases: the 'crhymes' they inspire (or used to inspire, in what I am

9

reactionary enough to call, without lowering my voice, the 'good old days'); the post-trial lives of the protagonists; the minutiae of investigations, such as the police lists, pathetic and surprising Salinger-parodies, of the contents of victims' and suspects' pockets.

But what fascinates me perhaps most of all is the way in which murder (other crimes, too, but murder especially) invests ordinary, everyday things with a terrible significance: the tatty raincoat in the Wallace case, the 'rising sun' postcard, the paper flowers in the recent McKay outrage. A murder is committed and suddenly these unimportant articles are transformed, are given a new and vital identity, become clues in an investigation, exhibits at a trial.

There is for me—and for others, I hope—a similar fascination to be found in much of the correspondence quoted in this book. Generally speaking, what I have tried to do is to use the correspondence connected with a case to throw fresh light—sometimes from a pretty obtuse angle, admittedly—on to the case itself. Although comparatively few of the letters can truly be termed *forensic* clues, nearly all of them, it seems to me, hold clues of one sort or another: clues to a possible cause of a crime, for instance, or to the feelings and thoughts of normal people caught up in abnormal situations.

Several of the letters are of a peripheral nature. They did not affect events; nor do they help in any substantial way to explain them. But they are, none the less, valuable—perhaps in the sense that they contribute to an appreciation of the atmosphere of a case, perhaps as unwitting self-portraits in pen and ink.

The temptation was always there, but in introducing the correspondence I have never—well, hardly ever—drawn conclusions from the messages or the styles of expression, for such inferences would be either so facile as to constitute a waste of space, or so subjective, and based on such fragile evidence, that the choice between accepting or rejecting them might as well be made by the toss of a coin. Epistolic divination has no place in criminology; its proper setting is a booth at the end of a seaside pier.

The letters included in this collection will remind aficionados of crime of other letters, equally apt, that I have had to leave out.

Probably the most conspicuous omissions are the letters of the two Smiths—Madeleine (who forms a threesome with Edith Thompson and Augusta Fullam, women whose letters to their lovers survived while their lovers' letters were destroyed) and George Joseph Smith (who, responding to an enquiry regarding his background from a solicitor acting for the family of one of his subsequent bath-night victims, began his letter: 'My mother was a Buss horse, my father a Cab driver, my sister a rough rider over the arctic regions—my brothers were all gallant sailors on a steam-roller.'). But if I had included these, and others like them, I should have finished up with a vast collection of letters, more appropriate to a mail-bag than to a book.

I have done my best to vary the types of letter and letter-writer, and to mix celebrated cases with a few that are less well known—maybe quite unknown to some readers.

My task has been eased by the help I have received from, among others, Sir James Dale Cassels, Basil Donne-Smith, Robert F. Hussey, and Richard Whittington-Egan. I am grateful to them.

1 Correspondence Course

From Lieutenant Henry Clark of the Indian Subordinate Medical Department, newly attached to the Station Hospital, Agra, to his wife Maud, living in Delhi, who had neglected to send him a leather case of hair brushes given to him by Mrs Augusta Fullam:

2 April 1911

If you cannot read and understand English please let me know, for then I can write to you either in Hindu or Bengali, as the case may be. . . . If you will take my advice you will either remain in Delhi, or proceed to Meerut, but please do not come here, for the day you place your foot in Agra, you may be quite sure I will promptly resign the service, as I am fed up with your low, disgusting ways, for I am quite sure you don't care a damn what becomes of me, so long as you draw Rs.200 a month. You can go wherever you like, but don't attempt to come near me, otherwise you will know the consequences immediately.
Trusting this will find you all quite well, as it leaves me the same, with fond love and kisses to self, and the rest at home.
I remain, Your affectionate Husband,

H. L. Clark

○○○○○

Two years before this dichotomous letter was written, in the summer of 1909, Clark, who was then aged forty, and his wife, six years his senior, had formed a friendship with the Fullams—forty-one-year-old Edward Fullam, a Deputy Examiner in the

Military Accounts Department, and his thirty-three-year-old wife 'Gussie'. Both families were Anglo-Indian. The Clarks had three grown-up children; the Fullams also had three children, all at school, and in 1910 Mrs Fullam gave birth to a fourth child, Myrtle.

Within a few weeks of their first meeting, Clark and Mrs Fullam were passionately in love. Although Mrs Fullam was not beautiful by contemporary standards, she had a fascinating personality, and it is hard to understand what attracted her—and kept her attracted—to Clark, an ugly, bullet-headed man with small, fleshy eyes, who lacked the social graces and was far from intelligent.

For the first eighteen months of the relationship, both Clark and Fullam were stationed in Meerut. When, in November 1910, Clark was transferred to Delhi, he frequently made the 40 mile trip to Meerut to spend a few illicit hours with Mrs Fullam, and they corresponded almost daily.

The thought of mutual divorce proceedings seems never to have entered their minds, probably because at this time—and especially in this place—divorce carried a stigma that would have ostracised Mrs Fullam from society and virtually destroyed Clark's already slim chances of promotion.

On 20 April 1911, soon after Clark had been transferred to Agra, 180 miles from Meerut, he visited Mrs Fullam and outlined a plan which, if successful, would leave them free to marry. The idea was simple: he would supply her—sometimes by hand but usually through the post—with arsenic 'tonic powders', and would provide a correspondence course on how to administer the powders to her husband; meanwhile, he would administer similar tonic powders to his wife, who, despite the threats contained in the letter already quoted, had joined him in Agra. Mrs Fullam was much taken with the plan, and the following day she wrote the first in a series of letters to Clark which forms a unique record of an attempt to murder by slow poisoning:

We now start afresh with a bright hope before us, shining like a beacon; our star of hope and comfort. So to the winds with trouble and care, darling.

14

The first few doses were too moderate, and, far from harming Fullam, actually had a beneficial—and aphrodisiac—effect:

24 April

I am sorry I was utterly unable, darling, to send you even a few lines on Saturday and Sunday, as I explained to you, Bucha [Hindustani for 'baby'] dearest, that I would have no chance, my hubby being at home. You are anxious to know about the 'tonic'. Well, sweetheart, darling, I have given it regularly since I last saw you, and I must say it is a good tonic, in very truth, darling. My hubby is quite well and strong, and it really seems to have done him good. I shall certainly continue it, lovie, and let you know later. How is Mrs Clark, your lawful wife? [This polite enquiry no doubt refers to the arsenical treatment Mrs Clark was receiving. Mrs Clark was far more suspicious of her husband than Fullam was of his wife, and Clark soon had to curtail the doses.]

Next day the first harmful symptoms developed, but they were not severe enough, and did not last long enough, for Mrs Fullam's liking:

26 April

Sweetheart mine, my hubby seems quite unaffected by the tonic powders. In fact, he is stronger and better than before, and more passionate, if such can be the case, in his case, my own darling. Some days I give him two, or even three powders, my Bucha dearest, but never less than one. I want you to let me know in return what you think of it, my own precious sweetie, and tell me how to go on?

At the beginning of May a fresh supply of powders arrived. Although Clark had increased the amount of arsenic, there was little change in Fullam's condition. Mrs Fullam became impatient:

28 April

Now, darling, you are very thoughtful in sending me some more powders. I was going to ask you for some, as I have only two left. Yesterday I gave my hubby three during the day, and he came back from the office at 6 p.m. with pains in his stomach, had a loose motion, and felt weak. He soon pulled up,

however, and now seems quite well, darling. I don't think
these powders are having any effect, Bucha. What do you
think, lovie? You say they must be given regularly, and then
you say you can't administer them to Mrs C. as regularly as
you would like to. Then what is the use of them, darling? She
will need much more than that, lovie. However, tell me plainly
what you think.

4 May

You will undoubtedly be glad to hear that I screwed up my
courage to give one powder yesterday, Harry darling, but no
effect so far, except as a very good tonic. I make my husband
very amorous, Bucha darling, and I don't want this, please.
Today another one will be administered, my sweetheart
darling, and you will know results.

5 May

Harry sweetheart, my hubby since yesterday has had slight
stomach trouble, and nausea, which he attributes to an attack
of indigestion, to which he is subject, darling. The powders
are going on being administered steadily, darling, but there is
little or no difference, except that my hubby feels the heat very
much, and complains of being tired. But that's an old story.
I wish to know, darling, please, in reply to this, how long I am
to continue the treatment, and when should desired results
appear, Bucha?

8 May

Now about the powders, Harry darling, I gave two on
Saturday, in two cups of tea, you know, as I send his tiffin.
But on Sundays only I never get a chance, Bucha. How many
hundreds of years will they take? I must say I don't approve
of your powders at all, darling. Meanwhile, we are constantly
running fearful risks, my own darling. However, if it please
you, then I am happy.

9 May

Of course, I have not yet received the tonic powders you
mention having sent, lovie, as I did not know anything about
them until I read your letter, so I did not inquire about the
tiny parcel at the P.O., but I suppose I shall get it tomorrow,

and will let you know, Harry darling, sweetheart mine. My
hubby is improving greatly on two of the old powders daily
(you remember five grains each). His complexion has changed
to a lovely pink, such as any young lady would envy, darling,
and he is full of life and vigour. . . . How long am I to
continue in this way. I think it would be much nicer to bring
about a crisis, soon.

Clark visited Mrs Fullam on 18 May, bringing with him some
new powders containing jalapin as well as arsenic, but they were
not at all successful:

23 May

Harry darling, my own precious Bucha, I have news for you,
and you must tell me how to act. I administered the full dose
in tea yesterday, but my hubby returned the whole jug of tea,
untasted, from the office, saying it was bad. When he came
home at six, I asked him why he had returned the tea, and he
said, 'There was some bad medicine in it,' so Harry darling, I
dare not continue with these powders. He also said, 'This is the
second time the tea has tasted bad,' which shows that the
jalapin is readily tasted.
My Bucha darling, Fate is against us, and all our plans are
utterly frustrated and have failed. What is to be done, darling?
I feel so very disappointed and downhearted, not so much on
my own account as on account of you, for I know darling you
want me so much, and the best prime years of your life are
being wasted, without love, care, and comfort, darling.
Now I want you to let me know two things in your reply,
please, Harry Bucha. Tell me what to do with the powders I
have by me, as I cannot give any more, for he can taste them,
darling. (2) What is your opinion or best plan of operation for
the future, my darling? It is an old saying, 'Love will ever find
a way,' or 'Where there's a will there's a way,' Harry darling,
so let me know exactly what you think. The first powders were
tasteless and unsuspected, but not strong enough, but these
jalapin ones do not suit at all, darling.

Ending this letter, Mrs Fullam took a roundabout route, via
the illness of a mutual acquaintance, to arrive at the suggestion
that a more potent powder was needed:

Poor old G. is very ill with acute pains in his stomach, Harry darling. He has three doctors attending, enough to kill anyone, I should say. One says gout in the stomach, another says gall-stones, and the third declares it's appendicitis; so let us see between them what they manage to do with the poor man's life, darling. Now this is written with all apologies to my dearest, sweetest darling old Dr. sahib, for, of course, there is none other so clever in my eyes, sweetheart. Harry, darling, as you are so clever, my darling pet, do consider and hit on a plan that will soon achieve our most desired and longed-for results; and darling, if there is anything you wish to send me in a small parcel, please register it.

In reply, Clark suggested that croton oil should be given 'by mistake' for castor oil, but Mrs Fullam turned down this idea at once:

26 May

Sweetheart, darling, I think your plan about the croton oil won't do, Bucha, because my husband seldom or never takes a dose of castor oil—he hates it. But I don't clearly understand you, my sweetie; you once say you are studying to take some other stuff, and then you say you can send me some more powders, if I let you know by return post. Darling sweet, have you decided on anything yet? And please do remember it must be tasteless, my Bucha. If my hubby were only in ill health, and I had to dose him at all, things would be very much easier, wouldn't they?

On 15 June, for the first time, Fullam's eyes became inflamed; this is a classic symptom of chronic arsenical poisoning, and is caused by the excretion of the poison through the lachrymal gland. On the same day Mrs Fullam received from Clark a far stronger dose of the poison, which she administered to her husband that night; had he not vomited most of the arsenic from his body, the dose would almost certainly have been fatal. Mrs Fullam kept Clark informed of this new development:

17 June

Since four p.m. [on the 16th]
        Vomited eight times, purged once.

Vomited ten times at a quarter to nine.
Vomited twelve times at ten p.m.
Slept after that.

17 June [second letter]

My husband has been very ill all Friday night, since four
o'clock, with symptoms of cholera. I got the Staff-Surgeon,
Captain P., to whom he is entitled, to treat him, and also
Captain W. has been kindly giving him help. I have been up all
night giving him ice, &c. My hubby declares his last mouthful
of tea and tiffin caused a burning sensation, and he started
reaching in office. My darling, I can't go to the P.O. this
morning for your dearest letter, sweetheart, as I can't leave
him, and I expect Captain P. any minute. They all blame the
Masonic dinner on Thursday night, but he himself says the
tiffin upset him, darling. You and I know how.

18 June

He is very weak, Harry darling, and lies for hours with eyes
closed, not speaking much or taking any notice of things. The
reaching has all stopped, but he complains of a soreness in his
stomach, and seems weak, as I tell you. Also rush of blood to
the head, and a headache.

21 June

Oh! I have been through such an awful time lately! This
week has seemed an eternity, and I have felt so lonely and
miserable. My hubby is sick; he does not improve at all since
that Friday night. He gets half a tonic powder every day, and
his liver seems affected. He takes all sorts of medicine, Harry
darling, and seems a different man. He now goes to the office
in the phaeton, and returns in it again for tiffin, after which he
sleeps till five, and then goes for a drive. Sweetheart darling, I
am acting on my own account entirely, as I have not received
your letter, and do not know what directions you gave me, or
anything. Anyhow, my own Bucha lovie, all for your sweet
sake! I am not happy, as the whole tone and trend of this
letter will show you, darling.

22 June

My hubby still continues ill. I have come here [the post

office] for a bottle of Sanatogen for him, darling. He has very bad dyspepsia, rush of blood to the head, insomnia and all, and he is talking of going up to Mussoorie on a few days' leave till the rains break.

24 June

Sweetheart mine, as you wish to know, I must tell you that the Staff-Surgeon did not exactly state his diagnosis of my hubby's illness last Friday night; the only remark he made was, 'Oh, Lord, you went to a Masonic Banquet last night,' and then he laughed. But Capt. W., the old duffer opposite, said the cause of such a severe illness was very strange, and when my hubby persistently told him of the scalding in his stomach as soon as he had swallowed the last mouthful of tea and tiffin, then he said, 'If you had any enemies, I should say you were poisoned with arsenic poisoning.' Harry darling, I firmly believe that my hubby suspects me because he said that the tiffin went to the office with some irritant poison in it. The whole thing has subsided and blown over now, Harry lovie, but you can imagine all I have gone through.

27 June

Sweetheart mine, as my hubby has gone again to the Cantonment General Hospital today, to see Lieut. Monroe, I take the opportunity of writing my letter, Harry darling, not knowing what the day may bring forth, as his eyes are ordered complete rest, and he is going to apply for ten days' leave. . . . Now, Harry darling, please let me know by return post, whether the tonic powder affects the eyes? I have an idea it does, lovie Bucha.

28 June

I give half a tonic powder every day in his Sanatogen, lovie darling, because it lays on the top of the white powder quite unsuspiciously, and he mixes it up in his teaspoon. I find, by boiling into a solution as you direct, Harry darling, the symptoms become much more severe as in Friday's case, darling, and there may be suspicion attached, having that scalding feeling down the throat. But this, in the Sanatogen, is a much easier way, don't you think, my Bucha darling? I told you I was doing my best, and you should trust me.

Fullam was given sick leave and on 3 July he travelled alone to the hill station of Mussoorie. While he was away, Clark spent four days with Mrs Fullam in Meerut—'four blissful days,' she called them. 'Neither of us can ever forget those happy hours and days together, nor do we wish to forget them, my own darling.' The start of the monsoon rains made Meerut hot and sticky, and there were many cases of heat-stroke. This gave the ingenious Mrs Fullam an idea, and on 11 July, the day before her husband's return, she wrote to Clark:

Harry, my own very precious sweetheart, I must mention to you that Mr N——, whom I think you know, got a heat-stroke evening before last, and is seriously ill. He is about my hubby's height and build, with the same florid complexion. Do you think, lovie darling, that the same symptoms could be produced on someone we know? Especially now, coming down from the Hills to Meerut, which is at present very hot. More especially, darling, as he was suffering from cerebral congestion long before he went up. Let me know what you think of this, and if it can be done without suspicion whatever?

Clark liked the idea, and decided to prescribe a mixture of atropine and cocaine. He must have shown some hesitancy, however, because on 14 July Mrs Fullam wrote to him:

Can you forget all about me, and turn your thoughts away from your girlie, Gussie Buchee, or do you think we should try and use the means of the heat-stroke, to be happy once again, darling love? . . . I have fully made up my mind about the heat-stroke affair. Even if you never marry me, I can suffer! So please send me the powder one day next week, when convenient to you, darling, under a registered cover, and addressed to Mrs Clarkson [her rather obvious *nom de meurtre*], as usual, and please let me know full instructions. Also how long after taking will the effect take place? He does not perspire so freely as you or I do, Bucha, but still there is slight moisture. His eyes are better, but still bloodshot.

The letters went back and forth, questions and answers, leading to the administration of the heat-stroke mixture:

18 July

Before you send me the liquid syrup containing the powder, write and let me know when to expect it. My hubby told me that one of the Hussar men had died of heat-stroke that very afternoon. So I asked him what sort of death it was, and he said: 'Oh, very easy; one of the easiest I know.' So I warned him not to go working in the garden as he does, morning and evening, his face getting quite red. Really, Harry darling, I don't know how he escapes getting heat-stroke. He gets amorous, but is weak. As you say, he is in a very favourable condition for it. His eyes are bloodshot still, as though he drank, and his face at times is almost purple. The only thing that keeps me back from doing it, my Bucha darling, is the thought of ways and means, and how to manage afterwards. . . . I do not give any tonic powders, darling, as he does not need them, and I have no chance to administer them. The liquid will be quite enough.

19 July

Thanks for letting me know in detail about the symptoms, darling. You know I have a very hard task before me. I am now anxious for your dear advice on all these matters, which torture my poor brain, day and night, darling. You can despatch the liquid by next Wednesday. I can call for the parcel personally, my own darling, as it will be risky sending it here.

25 July

Sweetheart mine, I have fully made up my mind to try and administer the liquid on Thursday night, the 27th, at dinner, and I have ordered the cook to prepare mullighitawny soup, darling, so that we will eat it with rice, and add lime juice. So my own Bucha lovie, if you disguise the bitter taste with lime juice, or salt, darling, it will go well with the acid soup, and raise no suspicion, darling. Besides, on Thursday afternoon, I think we will be going to the Berkshire Sports, held in front of your old Section Hospital, Bucha lovie. So, as it is so hot and steamy, without a drop of rain, he will be supposed to have got a touch of the sun that afternoon, darling. So I think Thursday will be the best day to finish off this dreadful business. Don't you agree with me, my darling?

I have no chance to put it in his lime juice and soda drinks, as

he opens the bottle and pours it out himself, lovie. He and I
both take Vermouth and lemonade at dinner, and if I had a
chance I would mix it up in that, but he mixes it all up
himself, so the only thing is the soup. I sincerely hope that no
suspicion of any kind will attach itself to me or you, my own
sweetie, and then after that, all will be plain sailing.

Mrs Fullam was as good as her word, and the mixture of
atropine and cocaine went into her husband's soup on the night
of Thursday, 27 July.

28 July
They have taken away my dear hubby to the Officers' Ward,
in the Station Hospital, after a most dreadful night, more like
a nightmare. He is raving with delirium, and quite unconscious.
I have just been to see him, 11.0 a.m., but find no
improvement. He has three orderlies looking after him, and
they have their work cut out to keep him down.

29 July
Today he is quite conscious. The fever is only 99, but he is
very weak. I am only allowed to stay two or three minutes at
his bedside, and he does not say much; he seems quite dazed.
I shall tell you, lovie, the whole thing from Thursday night, as
I would like you to know all, my own very precious lovie.
I mixed half the dose in his soup that night, but as soon as he
tasted it, he sent for the cook and abused him for making such
bad soup, so bitter and so full of mustard oil, as he called it,
Bucha darling. Anyhow, he had taken about a couple of
spoons, and about gunfire, when we were seated in the garden,
Harry darling, he complained of rush of blood to the head, and
asked me to pour cold water on his neck and hands, which I
did. Then I took his temperature, which was 99.6. So I said,
'Eddie, dear, you get into bed and I will give you a dose of
fever mixture.' So I mixed half of the remaining half into a
full dose of diaphoretic ['sweating mixture'], and took it to him
in the dark. He tasted it, and made a very wry face, saying, 'Is
that fever mixture?' I replied, 'Yes! you swallow it quick,' and
I brought the bottle and the lantern, and he sat up and read
the label, and also smelt the contents, after taking the dose. I
then said, 'Now go to sleep, and if you want anything you can
wake me.' My own precious lovie darling, we both fell asleep,

23

but I not very much, and at 2.30 a.m. he woke me up saying he felt very ill, and was getting paralysed. I called the ayah, and she and I sat chafing his hands and feet, lovie Bucha. But he asked me to send for Captain Weston, who came and said his heart was failing. Then by 4.0 a.m. he got worse, my own darling, so I sent the phaeton, and a line to Captain Keene. He came, but my husband was quite delirious. So Captain Keene decided to remove him into hospital at the first flush of daylight, because he said I would never manage him. I told you the three orderlies had their work cut out. He has been very seriously ill, Harry darling, and would have died had the first whole dose gone down. But it was not my fault, Bucha pet, the bitter taste was to blame, and not I, sweetie.

30 July

He is improving slowly but surely. . . . He is very comfortable, and is lying there with the ice bag continually on his head. They have diagnosed the case as heat-stroke.

31 July

My hubby is getting on slowly, but surely. The tingling sensations in his feet and hands are just passing off, and he has a normal temperature, only feels weak. The ice bag is still kept constantly on his head, darling, and when I go and see him he talks quite naturally.

Fullam's recuperative powers were quite remarkable. By 14 August he had partially recovered and was allowed to return home. On the same day Mrs Fullam wrote to Clark:

Everyone thinks they are doing a very foolish thing by sending him home so soon, as the heat is so great and there is fear of a relapse. It is so hard for me, Harry darling, and I only wish it was all over. You should pity and sympathise with me very much, my own darling. He is to continue the hospital mixture of quinine, pill and Mag. sulph. three times a day; also two baths daily and keep very cool.

Two days later the prophesy of a relapse was made to come true. According to Mrs Fullam's nine-year-old daughter Kathleen (giving evidence at the trial):

24

It was in the afternoon when he got ill the second time. He had some medicine. My mother gave it to him. My father was in the dressing-room when my mother gave him the medicine. He drank it, and after drinking it, he said to my mother, after a little while, 'Oh, Gus, you have given me the wrong medicine.' When he said that, my mother said that she did not think she had. He said that his throat and tongue were burning. He looked at his tongue in the glass. After that, he ran to his bed. Then he called out for someone to bring him some ice and water. My mother was by his bed, and my brother Frank, who is six, and I were in the drawing-room. There was just a door between. Then he was praying, and saying, 'Oh, God, have mercy on me.'

Captain Weston was called, and Fullam was rushed back to hospital. Yet again he resisted death; but the effort left him a hopeless invalid, and Mrs Fullam started to think in terms of poetic justice:

> 9 September
> My husband is very ill. I am the only one allowed to see him. He never speaks to me hardly, but just lies with his eyes closed. He can't walk, as you may suppose, nor can he even sit up, but just twitches, and jumps, and in the intervals stares like a lunatic. What a prospect! But I did it, and so I deserve a ruined life, and a broken home.

> 12 September
> I did not write the day before yesterday, dear, owing to little Myrtle [her twelve-months-old daughter] being ill. I went out on business, my darling, and fancy! she got hold of the bottle containing your famous liquid, which is so deadly certain, and luckily the cork was quite tight, but she sucked all round the cork and when I got home, I snatched it from the little pet, and scolded the ayah for unearthing things I had so carefully put away. Well, Myrtle soon became scarlet, and began to twitch a little, so I kept her in a cold bath and she gradually got better. But you can fancy my state of mind, Harry darling, and I really thought I would lose her. She must have got very little, thank God!

Early in September a medical board ordered Fullam's retirement from the Military Accounts Department. He and his family were offered free passage to England, and for a while Mrs Fullam was in the depths of despair, believing that the attempt to murder her husband was, by a vicious paradox, to be the cause of parting her from her lover forever.

Your kind, loving and welcome letter to hand safely this morning, for which many thanks, darling. It is only one of the few more letters I shall receive from my sweetest treasure, and then never more will I see the dear familiar handwriting with its firm, upward strokes, so determined and so characteristic of the beloved writer, darling!
What a shame that we two, who love each other so devotedly and passionately, must part, perhaps never to meet again in this wide world, lovie. Oh, it cannot be, it is not possible, surely. The blue sky and flowers during day, and the moon and stars by night, would all be darkness and chaos without your dear presence, Harry darling, my one and only love, my King. There is no more to say, Bucha. You are coming soon to see me, tonight you will be here, I shall see your dear face, touch your hands and face, and see you smile. But all that will make it so much harder! Oh, God give me strength to bear this cruel, bitter blow of parting, after all I have done. It is not my fault, Harry dearie, it is simply fate. I cannot write more.
Much fond love from your loving little sweetheart and Buchee darling.

Gussie
(Till death)

Then—for some unaccountable reason—Fullam decided that when he was released from hospital, he would spend his retirement at Agra. In a state of euphoria, Mrs Fullam rushed to the post office and sent a telegram to Clark, who was completely flummoxed by the sudden turn of events.

3 October

Lovie, dearest, you seem to be quite perplexed by my wire of yesterday afternoon, and I am sorry I worried you so. But I did get excited hearing . . . my hubby's sudden decision to go to Agra, that I rushed off and sent you that wire. I hope and trust you received my letter of explanation, my own darling, and I wonder if you can secure that little place in Metcalfe Road for us?

Sweetheart mine, I feel sure you will try and get a nice suitable place in Agra, because you would like immensely to have me near you, and this is such a good chance when he is so eager to go to Agra.

Fullam arrived in Agra, with his family, on 8 October. He died two nights later, on the 10th, after his wife had poisoned his dinner, and Clark, whom he had invited to share the meal, had executed the *coup de grâce* with an injection of the alkaloid poison, gelsemine. Before the injection was given, Kathleen Fullam went to her father's bedside:

Father said, 'I am going, Kathleen, dear. Be a good girl, and God will bless you. Give my love to Leonard [her brother], and tell him not to fret.' He then asked, 'Where's mother?' I replied, 'In the dining-room. Shall I go and call her?' Father said, 'No, dear. I do not want her.'

The funeral took place the following day, as is normal in India, and three days later Mrs Fullam wrote to Clark:

I know you will love to receive these few lines from me this morning, because you count it a privilege, I am sure, to get my handwriting. Sweetheart mine, I felt so happy and blissful last night when we parted and you called me your 'precious darling' and your 'Heart's own Queen'. Oh, darling, I retired to rest for the night so very happy and I thought to myself, 'My Harry loves me and cares for me with a deep, true, pure love, more than anyone else on earth has ever loved me.' How good it is, my own darling, to be so dearly loved by a strong, tender man, it is 'more precious than rubies'. Harry darling, sweetheart mine, you know what a dreadful, anxious time I have gone through lately, in fact, we both have gone through. Is it any wonder then that I should look pale and washed out, my sweetie? You don't look pale or tired, but much happier and contented, and the very picture of strong, vigorous manhood, and just what a fine, muscular, sunburnt doctor should be, lovie Bucha. Now please don't you worry about giving me a tonic. I am all right and quite happy, darling, and you are my best and only tonic. I never dreamt that I could ever be so happy in this life, my Bucha darling, and I hope one day we shall both be happier even than we are now. Sweetheart darling, let me now take this opportunity of thanking you very heartily for all your kindness to me and mine since coming to Agra. How very good and thoughtful you have been, my heart's treasure. Every little detail for our comfort has been planned and ordered by you, darling, and I have watched and noticed it all and loved you all the more.

ᴏ-ᴏ-ᴏ-ᴏ-ᴏ

Getting rid of Fullam was only half the plan. Now it was up to Clark to murder his wife. Months passed, and Mrs Fullam's letters to Clark contained more, and less, subtle reminders:

Sweetheart mine, what did Mrs C. have to say on your arrival home last night? . . . I am so sorry if you have got into any trouble and had her nagging tongue about your ears, my own lovie Bucha. Never mind, cheer up, my darling. With me it will all be so different; you will then know and realise what a true loving wife can make a home for a man.

A woman who truly loves asks but one question, whether he whom she loves gives her his heart in earnest, my own darling. Sweetheart mine, how things seem to be working together in bringing us two lovers nearer and dearer together.

The happy climax is still to come, darling, and let us hope and pray it will not be very far away, but will terminate in our happy union and long married life, always together, my beloved. I am quite sure we shall be very happy in our wedded life, my darling, for ours is a true love match, isn't it?

The final letter was written early in November 1912, when Mrs Clark was visiting her sons in Meerut:

Let us hope that when she returns, darling, our dearest hopes will be realised. Oh, how happy I should be!

On the night of Sunday, 17 November, three days after her return from Meerut, Mrs Clark was murdered in her bed by a gang of bazaar ruffians hired by her husband. The contrast between the two methods of murder—the slow poisoning of Edward Fullam, the hastily organised beating to death of Maud Clark—may be explained by the fact that in October 1912 Mrs Fullam had become pregnant.

Clark was suspected almost at once. Nature imitated art when the detective in charge of the investigation followed the example set by Sherlock Holmes and asked why the dog had not barked in the night; the answer, he discovered, was that Clark had locked the animal in an out-house. A clumsy attempt to simulate robbery only drew attention to the fact that nothing of value had been stolen.

The police arrested Clark on 18 November. The four hired killers—their leader an ex-servant of the Clarks—were arrested soon afterwards. On the morning of 19 November Mrs Fullam's house was searched, and Clark's despatch box was found beneath her bed; it was filled with the letters she had written to him. Mrs Fullam 'went very red and fell like a heap into a chair' when the box was opened. She, too, was taken into custody, and on 6 December her husband's body, well preserved by arsenic, was exhumed.

Mrs Fullam's solicitor advised her to petition to turn king's evidence, and a fortnight before she stood trial with Clark for the murder of her husband, she wrote to the Joint Magistrate:

Dear Sir—
I have been considering over my case, and feel perfectly
distracted and worried in mind, so much so that I feel it is my
duty in the sight of God, and for the sake of all justice and
truth, to turn 'King's Evidence' on both cases.
May I beg you, therefore, kindly to forward this my appeal to
the Honble. High Court, Allahabad, for due consideration.
I remain,
   dear sir,
Yours faithfully,
   A. Fullam

Allahabad.
12th February 1913.

To The Joint Magistrate

Dear Sir —

I have been considering over my case & feel perfectly distracted & worried in mind so much so that I feel it is my duty in the sight of God & for the sake of all justice & truth, to turn "King's Evidence" on both cases.

May I beg you therefore, kindly to forward this my appeal to the Honble High Court;

Allahabad, for due consideration.

I remain,
dear Sir,
Yours faithfully
A. Fullam

Letter written by Mrs Fullam while awaiting trial

This petition was ignored, and at two separate trials—first for the murder of Edward Fullam and then for the murder of Maud Clark—Mrs Fullam and Clark were found guilty of both charges. Clark was sentenced to death, but as Mrs Fullam was 'quick with child', her sentence was commuted to penal servitude for life. Of the four bazaar *badmashes* charged with murdering Mrs Clark, one was permitted to turn king's evidence, another was acquitted, and two were found guilty and sentenced to death.

Clark's last request before his execution was to be allowed to see Mrs Fullam. The authorities were willing to grant this, but she refused to meet him.

Mrs Fullam gave birth to Clark's child, a son, in July 1913. She died only ten months later. People who believe in the eye-for-an-eye concept of justice will be gratified to know that the cause of her death was heat-stroke.

31

2 Irene Munro

In most murder cases the emphasis on the victim's death obscures any picture of his or her life: the victim is a still figure, horizontal and coffin-shaped; a name around which an indictment is framed; a collection of parts, broken, poisoned or pierced, from which inferences are drawn by medico-legal experts. It is the murderers that come off best as far as posterity is concerned; very few victims are recalled as individuals, or have faces in the mind's eye, and most of these are remembered for the traits which contributed to, or provided, the motive for their murder. Of the innocent victims, one that emerges clearly from the transcript pages is Irene Violet Munro; she has been dead more than fifty years, yet one sees her as plainly as if she were a girl seen yesterday, walking in sunlight, with no reason to feel afraid.

In 1920, the year of her death, she was seventeen; she is said to have looked older but her photograph denies this. Dark and unremarkably pretty, with rather prominent teeth, she worked as a shorthand-typist for a firm of underwriters in Regent Street, London, earning £2.37½ (£2 7s 6d) a week. This was her second job since leaving school; she had previously been employed by a court bootmaker. An only child, she lived with her widowed mother, who was housekeeper to a family called Sinclair in South Kensington.

Early in the year, Irene and her closest friend, Ada Beasley, met a young Frenchman who worked in Regent Street. Unknown to her mother, Irene went out with him once or twice, sometimes in company with Ada Beasley, other times alone. On 20 March he wrote to her:

My darling Irene,
You naughty little girl to leave me by myself till Friday. I was
so hopeful to see you tomorrow. . . .
Never mind Ada. Don't tell her what we intend to do in the
future. It is so much nicer to be alone with you. But I am used
to keep my promises and I have booked three balcony stalls
for Saturday's matinee 'Chu Chin Chow'. Will you inform Ada
about this and arrange that we meet at exactly 2 o'clock in
front of the theatre? As for Friday I will book two seats for an
evening performance for you and me, and will meet you at
seven o'clock p.m. at the corner of Swan and Edgar's in Regent
Street before the first window. . . .
I enclose a pound note for you little bird to buy you some
things you may be in need of, and also would suggest you buy
at the chemist some Icilma cream to put every night on your
pretty face to render it clean and bright skin.
Hoping you are alright and not suffering any more from your
Sunday's sudden illness, I remain, dearest,
Yours very sincerely,

R.S.

Mrs Munro accidentally discovered this letter. She spoke to
her daughter about it and was told that it was just 'a little flirtation
between her and Ada'. The Frenchman continued to write, but
Irene at first invented excuses for not meeting him, then ignored
his letters. She may have done as her mother asked and returned
the pound note, but she kept another of his presents, telling Mrs
Munro that she had bought it herself. This present was a small
handbag of faded blue silk with a silk handle and a metal clasp.

⊖⊖⊖⊖⊖

On Friday, 13 August, Irene was told by her employer to start
her annual fortnight's holiday the following Monday. Mrs Munro
had already arranged to spend the same two weeks with relatives
at Portobello, near Edinburgh; she asked her daughter to accom-
pany her, but Irene said that she preferred the seaside. Next
morning, before seeing her mother off at Wapping Pier, she made
up her mind to go to Eastbourne.

On the Sunday she prepared her holiday things. These included an old black straw hat with a transparent brim, a light grey coat-frock with green silk tracing, two common crepe-de-chine dresses, a blue gabardine costume, a dressing jacket, four cotton blouses, white calico combinations with white lace insertion, a wool scarf, a nightdress case, eight handkerchiefs, three reels of thread, a thimble, a packet of needles, a Bible and two romantic novels.

She set off early on Monday morning, carrying a cheap fibre suitcase and her blue silk handbag. More concerned with looking smart than with wearing clothing appropriate to the season, she wore her Sunday-best coat of green wool with imitation fur twelve inches deep at the bottom and trimming the collar and cuffs.

As soon as she had found somewhere to stay in Eastbourne, she bought some picture postcards; one of these she sent to her mother, saying that she had arrived safely and giving her address, and the rest went to friends. To Ada Beasley she wrote:

Seaside, Eastbourne

Dearest Ada.— Arrived here today. Weather is absolutely gorgeous. (Better touch wood.) I'm not in love with Eastbourne yet, but of course I haven't been here a day, so I suppose I cannot really tell you what I think about it. Feeling terribly tired; got up at 5.30 this morning. Suppose you will be going down to Folkestone soon. Please write and let me know. Wish you were down here. Love,

Rene

On Thursday morning Irene received a letter from her mother:

43, Wellington Street,
Portobello,
N.B. [North Britain]

My dear Rennie,

I was so pleased to hear from you. Glad to hear you had got settled, and I hope you will be comfortable. I sent a letter to Manson Place [South Kensington]—I don't know if you got it—telling you I arrived all right. I do wish you had come with

34

me. I am having a good time in a quiet way. Granny was so disappointed at not seeing you. I am being treated awfully well, eating always. They are making such a fuss of me. Such a nice little comfortable cottage, with a small garden at the back, so nice, and everything so spotless and clean. A lovely piano. Mother has it. It is nice to have such comfort. I go up to Aunt Bessie every day. She has a lovely home. They were all so disappointed at not seeing you. Archie is such a nice man. He sent a telegram to you Monday morning to Manson Place. Did you get it? He wanted you to come on by train. He said he would pay your fare. Was it not good of him? Such a nice girl Lizzie, and little Archie. Grandmother has given me a nice dress gold ring for you. I think it would fit you. I have bought a nice sewing machine, a Singer's hand machine. Mother gave it to me, but I am giving her £2 for it as I would not take it for nothing as she had paid £5 15s. for it. It is in perfect order and will be very handy. I have found out now that there is not a boat until the 4th of September. There is one tomorrow and on Friday, and not one until the 4th after that, so I will write to Mrs S. and tell her that I will not be home before that time. Will get home on Sunday evening, the 5th. Aunt Bessie is awfully well off. The house that Granny is in is hers, although she never told me, and this aunt left four houses. She is a lucky one. Uncle Archie has £3 15s. a week and pension 10s. She has had such a lot of jewellery left her, cases of silver spoons and fish knives and forks. You would be surprised to see the beautiful home. Their room is furnished in oak all to match, and a lovely bathroom. The children dressed so nicely. The beach is just close to the house, and there is a lot of shops as it is a small town. I went to the pictures with Auntie Jessie last night as it was raining. Mother has given me a nice warm grey coat for the winter. I think you ought to write to Aunt Bessie. I think I am going to Uncle Robert's in Glasgow on Saturday. The weather is cold here just now. I hope you will be happy at Eastbourne. Tell me all about your lodgings. I think you will manage by yourself for a few days until my return. I hope you will not be too lonely. Get out in the air and mind and keep yourself warm. Put on your coat and have good food. Granny looks very young for her age. She is very active, goes for her own errands. She is a great talker. You would laugh. She is very kind and anxious to make you comfortable. I hope you will make out this scribble. Write and let me know all news. I am now going to Auntie Bessie. Lizzie plays the piano very well. She has been learning for three years. I will have a lot of luggage when I arrive, but I will book at the station what I cannot carry. Being a Sunday I don't want carrying a machine. Well, goodbye, hoping to see you soon. Granny and everyone sends their love to you. Your loving mother,

F. Munro

Send a long letter.

Irene replied at once:

393 Seaside, Eastbourne
Thursday

Dearest Mother,
I was so pleased to get your letter and am very glad to hear it is so lovely up there. I am writing this on the beach. The weather is simply gorgeous, though very windy in the morning, and I feel much better already.
I had a most awful job to get a room. They were full up everywhere, and after trudging about all day was compelled to take a room at 30s. a week. Terrible price, isn't it? but I couldn't get anything else. Even then they couldn't put me up for Monday night, and I had to stay somewhere else and paid 2s. 6d. It is of course a lovely room, looking to the front, with a piano. It is a pity in a way that you are not here as my room is large enough for two people.
I went to Beachey Head on Tuesday evening and lost myself. I didn't get back until nearly eleven o'clock. Yesterday I went to Pevensey Bay—walked there and back.
I have two pounds fifteen left, have paid £1 deposit on my room, so have still 10s. to pay, also fare back to London, so that really I have only £1 10s. left to pay for my rent and board next week, and the remainder of this week: so please do send me down as much as you can to reach me by Saturday as I shall only stay here for a week and shall try to get something cheaper for next week, and I should not like it to come when I am gone. I get awfully hungry down here. I think it must be the sea air.
The name of this road is just 'Seaside'. Isn't that funny? It is

ever such a long road, and I am a threepenny ride from the
station.

Goodbye for the present. Please give my love to Grannie,
Auntie Jessie, and everyone.

Your affectionate

Rene

A few hours after posting this letter, Irene Munro was savagely
murdered. Her body was found the following day, partially buried
on the Crumbles, a lonely stretch of shingle and grass running
between Eastbourne and Pevensey Bay. She was fully clothed.
Her straw hat was pulled over her battered face and weighted
down by stones. There was no sign of her blue silk handbag.

The 'Crumbles murder' made front page news. Several popular
newspapers were willing to sacrifice truth to sensation, and the
most disgraceful imputations were made against the dead girl:
the post-mortem examination revealed that she was not a virgin,
therefore she was a whore; as she had had a brief relationship
with a Frenchman, it followed that she had had affairs galore; she
had bought a cheap pen-case for someone she called 'uncle', and
it stood to reason that this man was just one of a string of elderly
lovers. Such journalistic sophistry must have tortured Mrs
Munro, whose shabby gentility extended to not carrying a sewing
machine on a Sunday.

While the press was suggesting that Irene Munro had been
killed by a 'London lover' and that her handbag had been stolen
for the secrets it contained, the Eastbourne police, assisted by
Scotland Yard officers, were collecting information about her
movements on the last afternoon of her life.

Several witnesses remembered seeing her in the vicinity of her
lodgings between 2 and 3 o'clock. She was walking in the
direction of the Crumbles in company with two young men, the
elder of whom was carrying a yellow stick surmounted with a
carving of a dog's head. Soon afterwards they were seen by a
Royal Navy stoker called William Putland and his friend Frederick Wells; Putland knew the two men by sight and recalled
seeing them with 'the girl in the green coat' the day before. 'To
pass away the time and to see what they would do', Putland and
Wells followed the trio as far as the Crumbles. Unfortunately,

Wells was a half-hearted voyeur; when the girl and her companions climbed under the fence by the railway line along the Crumbles, he turned back towards Eastbourne. His final memory of the incident was seeing the girl offering the men sweets or fruit from a paper bag. Putland hesitated a few moments by the fence, then, not liking the look of the dog's-head stick, ran to catch up with his friend. The last he saw of the girl, she had picked up a stray sandy kitten and was holding it in her arms and stroking it. She and the two men 'seemed to be quite jolly and were talking together'.

They were next seen a few minutes later by a gang of labourers who were sitting in a disused railway carriage that was used as a shelter. While the younger man waited arm in arm with the girl, the other man came to the door of the carriage and dropped the kitten inside. 'Here you are, here's a kitten for you,' he said. The three walked on towards Pevensey; when they were some distance away, one of the men turned back, waved, and shouted: 'Look after the kitten.' The railway labourers were the last people to see Irene Munro alive. Her body was discovered 500 yards from the carriage.

The police identified Irene Munro's companions as two local men, Jack Field and William Gray. Although only twenty, Field had several convictions, including one for robbery from his mother; since being discharged from the Royal Navy in February, he had been unemployed. Gray, who was twenty-eight, was born in South Africa of Scottish parents; he had come to England in 1916 with the South African Heavy Artillery and had married an Eastbourne girl, illiterate like himself. He had been out of work for twelve months, spending his small service pension on beer and cigarettes, and relying on his wife's earnings as a domestic servant to keep their home going. Gray had no criminal record, but this was only because his luck had held out; among other offences, he had committed rape and had stolen a purse from a girl, afterwards threatening to 'do her in' if she informed the police.

Field and Gray were tried for murder at Lewes Assizes in December. Their answer to the charge was a ramshackle alibi, easily disproved by the police.

While they were waiting to go up the steps to the dock for the verdict, Gray was heard to say to Field: 'I never thought we were going to be in this hole.' Field replied: 'On Irene Munro's coffin were the words "Thy will be done".'

The jury found both men guilty, but added the rider—an extraordinary one, considering the cold-blooded nature of the murder—that they should be recommended to mercy on the ground that 'the crime was not premeditated'.

Field and Gray appealed, each blaming the other for the murder, but neither the appeal nor the jury's recommendation was effective.

The killers of Irene Munro were carefully put to death on a chill, misty morning in February 1921. Few tears were shed, and there were no demonstrations.

3 Lonely Hearts

In November 1947 a practical joker wrote to 'Mother Dinene's Friendly Club for Lonely Hearts', asking for details of membership to be sent to twenty-seven-year-old Mrs Martha Beck, the superintendent of a home for crippled children at Pensacola, Florida. The joke had awful consequences, bringing together one of the most grotesque partnerships in criminal history, whose activities in a period of just over a year included perhaps as many as a dozen murders; it resulted in legal proceedings that are said to have cost the State of New York more than $1 million; its final effect was to send Martha Beck and her partner, a Hawaiian-born Spanish-American called Raymond Fernandez, to the electric chair at Sing Sing Prison. Few jokes can have fallen flatter than this one.

❂❂❂❂❂

Martha Beck was not a pretty sight. Her obese body was supported by matchstick-thin legs; her face, heavily made-up, was cushioned on layers of chins and surmounted by a mop of coarse black hair. A series of childhood traumas, culminating in her being raped by an elder brother when she was thirteen, developed a dichotomy within her: she was both obsessed with, and repelled by, sex. On leaving school she decided to take up nursing, and applied for admission to the Pensacola School of Nursing:

> Some girls may write page after page telling why they chose
> the nursing profession. I feel that I can say why I chose this
> profession in a few words.
> I chose this profession, for, in this field of endeavour I sincerely

believe that I can do my best to aid humanity. I chose this profession without thought of self and want to prepare myself for this profession, not for material gains but for the purpose of aiding humanity and rendering services to others.

On the recommendation of her high-school principal, she was accepted without hesitation, and in 1942 she passed the state nurse's examination, gaining the highest marks in her class. But despite her qualifications, and despite the shortage of nurses (this was wartime, remember), she was turned down for job after job, invariably on account of her unpleasant appearance. When, at last, she obtained employment, it was with a seemingly pudibund undertaker, who hired her to deal with female corpses, washing, embalming and preparing them for burial. At least the job paid reasonably well. After a few months she had saved enough money to go to California, where the shortage of trained nurses was so acute that even an ugly, top-heavy girl like her could find employment. She returned to Pensacola in 1944, to work first of all at a maternity hospital (from which she was dismissed after a few months for entertaining a man in her room) and then at the home for crippled children. She now had two children of her own: an illegitimate daughter, the father of whom had threatened suicide rather than marry Martha, and a baby son, product of her brief marriage to a bus driver.

When Martha Beck received the 'Lonely Hearts' brochure she realised that her name had been sent to the club as a practical joke. But instead of throwing the brochure away, she examined the smeared pictures of anonymous women who were said to have found husbands and happiness through the club, and read and re-read the 'unsolicited testimonials' and the puff:

Mother Dinene has helped hundreds of women to find suitable mates, carefully selected from her long list of lonely but eligible men who are seeking—even as you are seeking—to find true happiness in a blissful marriage. Many of the men on her list are gay, witty, charming, and have good positions or are independently wealthy. Why should you not meet such men?

Why not, indeed? Martha Beck wrote to the club at once,

41

giving her true age—but not mentioning her excessive weight or her two children—and saying that she was always being told that she was 'witty, vivacious, and oozed personality'. Then, enclosing $5 for membership, she posted the letter and eagerly awaited results.

She did not have to wait long. The description she had given was circulated to male members of the club, and within a few days she received a letter from Raymond Fernandez in New York. She replied by return of post, and from then until shortly before Christmas they corresponded regularly, with Fernandez's letters waxing more lyrical and becoming more emotional all the time: he had been guided to her, he said, by a 'psychic power'; they had never met on the physical plane but their souls had 'been in love since the dawn of creation'. On 22 December Fernandez wrote that he was coming to Pensacola; before she could put him off, a telegram came saying that he was on the way and would arrive on the 28th.

Raymond Fernandez was a tall, thin man with a diminutive moustache emphasising full, some might say sensuous, lips; a dark wig covered his prematurely bald head, but still he looked a lot older than his thirty-four years. 'Like a rather seedy Charles Boyer' is how one acquaintance described him. During the war he had worked for British Intelligence in Spain, and had received commendations for courage. Until two years before his first meeting with Martha Beck he had led a useful and honest life; as a boy he had been convicted of stealing chickens, but this was his only brush with the law. Then, in 1945, a head injury sustained on board the ship bringing him back to the United States appears to have caused a personality change, and he became a full-time criminal. After serving a six months prison sentence for theft he joined several correspondence clubs and matrimonial bureaux, and combined pleasure with business by sleeping with and then swindling many of the women to whom he was introduced. When he made the trip to Pensacola he was thinking of Martha Beck as a prospective victim rather than as a possible wife.

Fernandez must have had a nasty shock when he saw Martha Beck in the flesh; but it was a far worse shock to learn that she had two young children and very little money. After spending two days and nights with her, Fernandez concocted an excuse for returning to New York. Martha wrote to him again and again, expressing her undying love, then received a curt letter calling the whole thing off; her reaction was a clumsy attempt to gas herself. Someone—probably Martha herself—forwarded the suicide note to Fernandez and he, alarmed that the suicide attempt might bring about police inquiries, wrote to her, begging her forgiveness and inviting her to stay with him for a while in New York. Martha did not have to be asked twice; she obtained a fortnight's leave, scraped together the fares for herself and the children, and set off. When the two weeks were up, Fernandez insisted that she return to Pensacola and, when she pleaded to stay, told her that he was already married; he put her on the train, thinking for the second time that he had seen the last of her. But when Martha returned to the home for crippled children she was told that her services were no longer required; no reason was given for the dismissal, but it seems likely that gossip about her affair with Fernandez had reached the ears of the governors of the home. A few days later Martha packed her few belongings, dressed the children and returned to Fernandez.

It appears that Fernandez decided to make the best of a bad job. He explained to Martha how he earned his living by swindling lovelorn women, and suggested that she should pose as his sister, thus aiding his 'cover'. She agreed in a flash. She also agreed that her children were 'an inconvenience'; they were sent back to Pensacola for her mother to look after.

The partnership prospered. For the next eleven months Fernandez travelled about the United States meeting female members of 'lonely hearts' clubs, introducing them to his 'sister', fleecing them, and then disappearing. Martha's jealousy was sometimes a problem (after Fernandez had married a woman in Arkansas, Martha insisted on sleeping with her during the honeymoon), but her usefulness and resourcefulness far outweighed her shortcomings; before long, Fernandez was as much in love with her as she was with him.

◦◦◦◦◦

Soon after Christmas 1948 Fernandez and Martha Beck introduced themselves as brother and sister to Mrs Janet Fay, an elderly widow living at Albany, the state capital of New York. Within a couple of days they were living in Mrs Fay's one-room flat, with Fernandez sleeping on a couch and the two women sharing the bed. A day or so later Mrs Fay (who should have known better, as she had been swindled by a 'lonely hearts' suitor only a year before) withdrew most of her savings, taking nearly $3,000 in cash and the rest in cheques payable to herself. As soon as the money was collected, Fernandez and Martha used a car stolen from an earlier victim to take Mrs Fay to a flat they had rented on Long Island. Mrs Fay wanted to inform her relatives of her impending marriage, so Fernandez wrote 'Surprise' on several sheets of notepaper and persuaded her to sign her name at the bottom of each sheet; the idea, he explained nudgingly, was to whet the relatives' curiosity: he would send off the cryptic, mystifying notes, and Mrs Fay could write fully as soon as they were married.

A few hours later Mrs Fay was beaten to death with a balpeen hammer; the evidence is unclear as to whether she was murdered by Fernandez or Martha Beck. Her body was placed in a trunk, and, after a long, almost farcical search for a suitable resting place, Fernandez rented a house in the Queens district of New York City and buried the body in the cellar. He and Martha then erased the word 'Surprise' from the sheets of notepaper, typed messages over Mrs Fay's signatures, and posted the fabricated letters to the dead woman's relatives. The letter to her stepdaughter was composed with especial care:

Dear Mary,
I am all excited and having the time of my life. I never felt as happy before. I soon will be Mrs Martin and will go to Florida. ['Charles Martin' was Fernandez's favourite alias.]
Mary, I am about to ask you a great favour. I would like you to call on the American Express Agency and have them ship my trunks and boxes that I have there to me. The address is on the various stickers I am enclosing in the letter.
I would like to sort out many things before I leave for Florida.

44

I am so happy and contented, for Charles is so good and nice to me and also his family. They have done everything to make me feel comfortable and at home.

I will close now with my best wishes for you both and love and kisses for the children. I really do miss you all but I am sure that my prayers are granted to me by sending me this wonderful man.

God bless you all,

Janet J. Fay

Far from putting the step-daughter's mind at rest, this letter only aroused her suspicions. Although the content was a fair imitation of Mrs Fay's epistolic style, the typewriting was far too expert to be the work of someone who had never used a typewriter in her life. The step-daughter was so uneasy that she reported Mrs Fay to the police as a missing person.

〇〇〇〇〇

On the day that Mrs Fay was murdered, Fernandez had received a letter from Mrs Delphine Downing, a widow with a two-year-old daughter, who lived at Grand Rapids, Michigan:

Dear Charles,

Thank you for your thoughtful Christmas greetings.

Christmas is so busy with its hustle and bustle and the lull afterwards is such a letdown. It gives me an empty, lonely feeling.

New Year's Eve I kept the neighbours' children so they could go out and the children were sleeping quietly when the whistles blew. The only noise was when a dog set up a noise at midnight.

I've been having trouble with my old car. Maybe I should have taken the advice and bought a new one, but I need to spend so much when it could be invested for Rainelle to use later.

I have a nice two-stall garage, but when I cleaned up the shop [a work-room] the tools and things filled it. But gradually I am getting everything sold.

Rainelle got a tricycle from some friends and she is sitting on it now and really making a noise. Do you like children's

carols? I hope you do, for if we continue to correspond, I will
mention Rainelle often.
I hope I don't break the rules of our friendship correspondence
by writing you before I give you time to consider my last letter.
Sincerely.

Delphine

Fernandez and Martha Beck arrived in Grand Rapids towards
the end of January 1949. Mrs Downing invited them to stay at
her house, and before long she and Fernandez were on terms of
sexual intimacy. Younger and more attractive than most of the
earlier victims, Mrs Downing was no less gullible—at first, that
is. She accepted his proposal of marriage and began to transfer
her property into cash assets—then, catching a glimpse of him
without his wig, she accused him of deceit and threatened to call
off the marriage. Another crisis arose when her menstrual period
became overdue; convinced that she was pregnant, she appealed
to Martha, the trained nurse, for help. Martha purchased a form
of sedative and—perhaps unintentionally, almost certainly not—
gave her an overdose. Mrs Downing began to menstruate almost
at once, but soon afterwards became extremely drowsy and had
to be helped to bed. The child, Rainelle, began to cry, and
Martha, her nerves on edge, seized her by the throat and tried to
choke her; she would no doubt have succeeded had not Fernandez pulled the child free. Fearing that when Mrs Downing
awoke and noticed the marks on Rainelle's throat she would go
to the police, Fernandez could think of only one solution: he shot
Mrs Downing in the head and buried her body in the cellar. The
following day he took the child down to the cellar, drowned her
in a washtub of stagnant water, and buried her beside her mother.

After the alarums and exertions of the last few days, Fernandez
and Martha Beck felt in need of a little relaxation, so they went
to see a film at a nearby cinema. While they were away, several
neighbours, suspicious at the sudden disappearance of Mrs
Downing and her daughter, telephoned the police. Fernandez
and Martha Beck returned to the house to find two detectives
waiting with a search warrant.

With the discovery of the bodies in the cellar, Fernandez

became loquacious and gave the police minute details of earlier crimes; whatever her partner said, Martha Beck confirmed. Information regarding the murder of Janet Fay was sent to the New York police and her body was recovered from the cellar at Queens. There had certainly been other murders (there was, for instance, virtually conclusive evidence that an Arkansas woman had been poisoned with barbiturates), but the authorities decided that it would be an impossible task to trace all the women who had had affairs with Fernandez and were now reported missing.

Michigan had no death penalty—New York did; so, after a brief legal struggle, Fernandez and Martha Beck were extradicted to New York to stand trial for the murder of Mrs Fay. They both pleaded insanity, and the trial, which dragged on for forty-four days, increased the wealth of a number of psychiatrists, most of whom knew precious little about the workings of the human mind but were expert at stringing together jargon phrases to produce verbose, high-flown gobbledygook. Found guilty of murder in the first degree, Fernandez and Martha Beck were sentenced to death and taken to Sing Sing Prison, where they were housed in opposite wings of 'The Centre', the building containing the condemned cells and the electric chair.

From her cell window Martha Beck was able to see Fernandez and to shout sweet nothings to him when he was taken to the exercise yard each day. They were allowed to write to one another, and her letters reveal her dependance upon Fernandez and her fear—teased by reports in newspapers and within the prison—that, as she put it, he was 'going to turn State's evidence and testify against me'. In her first letter, referring to the appeal against the New York verdict and the attempt to secure priority for the Downing murders, which would have meant a fresh trial in Michigan, she wrote to 'dearest Raymond':

Martha is not getting on the stand again if we have a new trial. I don't want a new trial if we have to cut each other's throats. Nor do I want one if it means you will refuse to look at me, smile, or speak when possible. I can take everything except a cold shoulder from you. . . .
I am glad you waved this a.m. Thanks, darling, from the

bottom of my heart. Ray—please, Ray—accept these flowers
and my love.
Your own Birdbrain.
P.S. If you don't return the flowers, I'll know you added my
initials to the bow knot, joining our love together with a tie so
tight that nothing can break it.

The flowers, it seems, were not returned. In her next letter she
referred to the birds she could see from her window:

Maybe I can train them, darling, to fly to you with a message
of love, for I never want you to forget that I love you. To me
you will always be the man I love. . . .
xxxxxxxxxx
xxxxxxxxxx
xxxxxxxxxx (If only I could deliver them in person!)

When they had been at Sing Sing for just over a month Martha
heard a rumour that Fernandez was thinking of 'doing a double-
cross'. She complained:

Why do they tell us things to make us hate each other? Just
because I heard such stuff is no sign I believe it. No one,
other than yourself, will ever make me believe that you would
turn against me. Now or ever—if I ever find out you have
turned against me, I would welcome death, for having loved
and trusted you always, I would rather die than live and know
that you had turned against me.

Even the psychiatrists who gave evidence at the trial could not
have gone far wrong in deducing something from a later letter:

I had a terrible dream. I dreamed that —— called me to the
gate to watch you. He wanted me to see that E. had come to
see you and they had locked her in a cage with you. Your arms
were about her, your lips on hers. . . . It hurt me. I turned
away and when I turned—bang—Martha hit the floor.

As the months passed, and as one legal stratagem after another
failed to rescind the jury's verdict, only prolonging the agony,

Martha Beck was unable to withstand the subtle torture of rumour. In one letter to Fernandez she accused him of saying 'vulgar and insulting things' about her, and went on:

> You are a double-crossing, two-timing skunk. I learn now that you have been doing quite a bit of talking to everyone. It's nice to learn what a terrible murderous person I am, while you are such a misunderstood, white-haired boy, caught in the clutches of a female vampire. It was also nice to know that all of the love letters you wrote 'from your heart' were written with a hand shaking with laughter at me for being such a gullible fool as to believe them.
> Don't waste your time or energy trying to hide from view in church from now on, for I won't even look your way—the halo over your righteous head might blind me. May God have mercy on your soul.
>
> M. J. Beck

But—such was the seesaw of her emotions—a few days later she wrote him a long letter, most of it too passionate to be printable, in which she apologised for not wearing white, his favourite colour, and told him more than once: 'This doesn't mean I don't love you.'

There were no rumours to shake Martha Beck's love for Fernandez, or his for her, on the night of Thursday, 8 March 1951, seventeen months after the trial. He went first to the electric chair; as he was strapped in, he pulled up his trousers so as to preserve the crease. Martha Beck entered the death chamber twelve minutes later. Although she had lost some weight while in prison, she had difficulty in squeezing into the chair. When the mask was about to be drawn over her face, a nervous tic lifted the corner of her mouth, giving the appearance of a lopsided grin. Next morning, the New York *Daily News* headlined the report of the executions:

HEARTS KILLERS
DIE IN CHAIR
MARTHA GOES WITH SMILE, WINK

✪✪✪✪✪

The following letter, written by Martha Beck to a Dr Richard
Hoffmann, will give consolation to those who insist on believing
that no one, not even the most cold-blooded multicide, is wholly
without virtue:

> Will you be so kind as to write to my mother and advise her
> how and what to tell my children about me? My daughter will
> be six in Sept., and will also start school the same month. You
> know, Dr. H., she already has two strikes against her and if I
> go to the chair it will be strike three. I feel that you are in a
> position to know how to tell her so that her little mind can
> grasp the truth and not be warped by all of the malicious jeers
> and gossip that she will have to face in the future. . . .
>
> Martha Beck—108594

4 Young England

It is no more than slight exaggeration (if, indeed, it is exaggeration
at all) to say that the course of history is changed more noticeably
by nonentities than by statesmen and soldiers: by people like
Lee Harvey Oswald, Van der Lubbe, Charles Guiteau, and, most
momentous nonentities of this century, the young men at Sara-
jevo.

Edward Oxford, an eighteen-year-old London barman, would
have been of that number had his aim been half as firm as his
purpose; as it is, his name is rarely enlarged above six-point type
in volumes of Victorian history.

In the early evening of Wednesday, 10 June 1840, as was her
custom, the young Queen Victoria, accompanied by the Prince
Consort, went for a pre-dinner drive in a low, open carriage. As
the carriage was driven up Constitution Hill, Edward Oxford,
standing by the railings of Green Park, drew a pistol from his
breast and fired at the Queen.

The providence of God averted the blow from her Majesty [said
the Attorney-General at the trial]. The ball was heard to whizz by
on the opposite side. . . . The carriage proceeded. The prisoner
then looked back to see if anyone was near to perceive him; he
drew another pistol from his breast, whether with his right hand
or his left is uncertain, and aimed at her Majesty. It would appear
that her Majesty saw him fire, because she stooped down. Again
the providence of God interfered. The prisoner fired, the ball was
heard to whizz on the other side—her Majesty escaped.

In the initial confusion a passer-by who had snatched the
pistols from Oxford was thought to be the offender, and (again

Edward Oxford shooting at Queen Victoria—a drawing by 'Phiz'

according to the Attorney-General) 'the parties around said, "You confounded rascal, how dare you shoot at our Queen?" ' But Oxford was determined not to have his thunder stolen by an imposter: 'It was I,' he hastily declaimed. This was not easy to believe, for he looked even younger than eighteen and not in the least bit lethal.

Corroboration of Oxford's statement was found in his lodgings in West Square, Elephant and Castle: a box containing arms and ammunition, and—far more alarming—three letters and a sheet of paper headed 'YOUNG ENGLAND'.

Beneath this title, neatly handwritten, were eleven rules for membership of what sounded like a large and dedicated subversive organisation. Most of the rules were decidedly esoteric, and the last was of a mind-bending ingenuity that can best be described as Kafka-cum-Carrollesque.

1. That every member shall be provided with a brace of pistols, a sword, a rifle, and a dagger. The two latter to be kept at the committee-room.
2. That every member must, on entering, take the oath of allegiance to be true to the cause he has joined.
3. That every member must, on entering the house, give a signal to the sentry.
4. That every officer shall have a factitious name. His right name and address to be kept with the secretary.
5. That every member shall, when he is ordered to meet, be armed with a brace of pistols (loaded) and a sword to repel any attack; and also be provided with a black crape cap, to cover his face with—his marks of distinction outside.
6. That whenever any member wishes to introduce any new member, he must give satisfactory accounts of him to their superiors, and from thence to the council.
7. Any member who can procure an hundred men shall be promoted to the rank of captain.
8. Any member holding communications with any country agents must instantly forward the intelligence to the secretary.
9. That whenever any member is ordered down the country or abroad, he must take various disguises with him (as the labourer, the mechanic, and the gentleman), all of which he can obtain at the committee-room.

10. That any member wishing to absent himself for more than one month must obtain leave from the commander-in-chief.

11. That no member will be allowed to speak during any debate, nor allowed to ask more than two questions.

All the printed rules to be kept at the committee-room.

LIST OF PRINCIPAL MEMBERS
FACTITIOUS NAMES

President—Gowrie.	*Council*—Ethelred.	*Captains*—Oxonian.
Justinian.	Ferdinand.	Mildon.
Aloman.	Nicholas.	Louis.
Coloman.	Gregory.	Amadeus.
Kenneth.	*Generals*—Frederic. *Lieuts.*	—Hercules.
Godfrey.	Augustus.	Neptune.
Council —Hanibal.	Othoe.	Mars.
Ernest.	Anthony.	Albert.
Augustin.		

MARKS OF DISTINCTION

Counsil—A large white cockade.　*President*—A black bow.
General—Three red bows.　*Captain*—Two red bows.
Lieutenant—One red bow.

A. W. Smith, *Secretary*

The three letters found at Oxford's lodgings read as follows:

Young England, May 16, 1839

Sir,

Our commander-in-chief was very glad to find that you answered his questions in such a straight-forward manner; you will be wanted to attend on the 21st of this month, as we expect one of the country agents in town on business of importance. Be sure and attend.

A. W. Smith, Secretary

P.S. You must not take any notice to the boy, nor ask him any questions.

Addressed—Mr Oxford, at Mr Minton's, High-street, Marylebone.

Young England, Nov. 14, 1839

Sir,

I am very glad to hear that you improve so much in your speeches. Your speech the last time you were here was beautiful. There was another one introduced last night by Lieutenant Mars, a fine tall, gentlemanly-looking fellow, and it is said that he is a military officer, but his name has not yet transpired. Soon after he was introduced, we were alarmed by a violent knocking at the door; in an instant our faces were covered, we cocked our pistols, and with drawn swords stood waiting to receive the enemy. While one stood over the fire with the papers, another stood with lighted torch to fire the house. We sent the old woman to open the door, and it proved to be some little boys who knocked at the door and ran away.

A. W. Smith, Secretary

You must attend on Wednesday next.

Addressed—Mr Oxford, at Mr Farr's, Hat and Feathers, Goswell-street.

Young England, April 3, 1840

Sir,

You are requested to attend tonight, as there is an extraordinary meeting to be holden, in consequence of having some communications of an important nature from Hanover. You must attend, and if your master will not give you leave, you must come in defiance of him.

A. W. Smith, Secretary

Addressed—Mr Oxford, at Mr Robinson's, Hog-in-the-Pound, Oxford Street.

The letters and the 'Young England' membership rules went a long way towards establishing that Oxford had fired the shots at the queen; as they were all in his own handwriting, they went just as far, perhaps further, towards establishing that he was not responsible for his actions.

After a two-day trial, which Oxford clearly enjoyed (he stopped smiling only to laugh out loud), the jury acquitted him on the ground of insanity. He was ordered to be detained during the pleasure of his intended victim, and was subsequently conveyed to Bedlam.

5 Mr Fox

Looking through the records of kidnapping cases, one is struck by the number of times that the criminal is either mentally abnormal or a first-generation immigrant. Indeed, these two conditions often go together, with an inherent *folie de grandeur* being aggravated and swollen by a craving for the affluence that motivated the move to a strange country. To cite just two examples, in the most famous United States case, Charles Lindbergh, jnr, was kidnapped and murdered by Bruno Hauptmann, a paranoid illegal immigrant from Germany, and in the sole British case, Mrs Muriel McKay was kidnapped and murdered by the West Indian brothers, Arthur and Nizamodeen Hosein, the elder of whom numbered among his several aberrations a desperate desire to be a country squire, while the younger was almost certainly schizophrenic.

Kidnapping is such a disgusting crime that one tends to ascribe an equal degree of loathsomeness to all kidnappers; but, in detail, some crimes are more disgusting than others. If, in the unlikely event of having nothing better to do, one were to compile a roster of kidnappers in order of contemptibility, there is little doubt the name of Edward Hickman would head the list.

ଠଠଠଠଠ

Early in December 1927, Hickman, a diminutive, curly-haired youth of twenty, planned the kidnapping of Marian and Marjorie Parker, the twelve-year-old twin daughters of a prosperous Los Angeles banker. On the day chosen for the abduction, however, a slight illness kept Marjorie at home, and Marian went to school

56

alone. In the afternoon, Hickman parked his car beside the playground of the Mount Vernon Junior High-School; when Marian Parker appeared, he called to her: 'There's trouble at home. Your father sent me to get you.' Without questioning the summons, the child got into the car and was driven away.

Hickman took her to a cheap apartment and forced her to write a letter at his dictation:

Dear Daddy and Mother:
I wish I could come home.
I think I'll die if I have to be like this much longer.
Wont someone tell me why all this had to happen to me.
Daddy please do what the man tells your or he'll kill me if you don't.

Your loving daughter
Marian Parker

P.S. Please Daddy.
　　I want to come home tonight.

The Parkers received Marian's letter by the following morning's post. Enclosed with the letter was a ransom note, the first of many, all of which were characterised by the word 'DEATH' meticulously penned in an obscure script at the top of the sheet; each note was signed either 'Mr Fox' or 'FATE'. The first note, demanding $1,500 for the return of the child, was passed to the police, who had been called to the house the previous day when Marian failed to return from school. Parker received a telephone call in the afternoon telling him where, when and how to hand over the money. Dozens of detectives were concealed nearby when Parker arrived at the appointed rendezvous; he waited for hours but the kidnapper did not turn up. Next day a second note accused Parker: 'You gave me your word of honour . . . not to tip the police. . . . You lied.'

The torture of the Parkers continued and was intensified. Every day at least one note arrived; several of the notes contained references to neighbours and to Parker's business routine, sug-

Dear Daddy and Mother:

I wish I could come home.
I think I'll die if I have to
be like this much longer.
Wont someone tell me why
all this had to happen to me.
Daddy please do what the
man tells your or he'll kill
me if youdon't.

Your loving daughter
Marion Parker.

P.S. Please Daddy.
I want to come home tonight

Marian Parker's letter to her parents

gesting that 'Mr Fox' possessed an uncanny power to see without being seen. One note read:

DEATH

P. M. PARKER:
FOX IS MY NAME. VERY SLY YOU KNOW. ∴
SET NO TRAPS. I'LL WATCH FOR THEM.

ALL THE INSIDE GUYS, EVEN YOUR NEIGHBO ISADORE B., KNOW THAT WHEN YOU PLAY WITH FIRE THERE IS CAUSE FOR BURNS. NOT W. J. BURNS AND HIS SHADOWERS [a detective agency] EITHER—REMEMBER THAT.

GET THIS STRAIGHT: YOUR DAUGHTER'S LIFE HANGS BY A THREAD AND I HAVE A GILLETTE READY AND ABLE TO HANDLE THE SITUATION.

THIS IS BUSINESS. DO YOU WANT THE GIRL OR THE 15 $100 GOLD CERTIFICATES US CURRENCY? YOU CANT HAVE BOTH AND THERE'S NO OTHER WAY OUT. BELIEVE THIS, AND ACT ACCORDINGLY. BEFORE THE DAY'S OVER I'LL FIND OUT HOW YOU STAND.

I AM DOING A SOLO SO FIGURE ON MEETING THE TERMS OF MR FOX OR ELSE.

FATE.

In a subsequent note, a postscript expressed the kidnapper's belief in his own omnipotence:

DEATH

P. M. PARKER:
Use good judgment. You are the loser. Do This. Secure 75 $20 gold certificates—US Currency—1500 dollars—at once. KEEP THEM ON YOUR PERSON. GO ABOUT YOUR DAILY BUSINESS AS USUAL. LEAVE OUT POLICE AND DETECTIVES. MAKE NO PUBLIC NOTICE. KEEP THIS AFFAIR PRIVATE. MAKE NO SEARCH. Fullfilling these terms with the transfer of the currency will secure the return of the girl.
FAILURE TO COMPLY WITH THESE REQUESTS MEANS—NO ONE WILL EVER SEE THE GIRL AGAIN.

EXCEPT THE ANGELS IN HEAVEN. [The word 'heaven' was circled with dashes to give a shining effect.]
The affair must end one way or the other within 3 days.
72 HRS.
YOU WILL RECEIVE FURTHER NOTICE.
But the terms Remain the Same.

FATE

IF YOU WANT AID AGAINST ME ASK GOD NOT MAN.

After receiving this note, Parker decided to keep his dealings with 'Mr Fox' secret from the police, and when the softly spoken kidnapper telephoned again, agreed to meet him at a car park that evening.

Parker drove up beside Hickman's car. He could dimly see his daughter wrapped in a blanket at the young man's side; her face was visible, and she appeared to be drugged. 'Give me the money and I'll leave her down the road a way,' Hickman said. Parker threw the money into the car, and Hickman drove off, stopping after a few hundred yards to place the wrapped body on the ground.

Parker found the child dead. The arms and legs had been severed with a pocket knife; the eyelids were sewn open. A post-mortem examination revealed that the child had been strangled, but, according to the pathologist, she had died of sheer fright before the attack.

The limbs were found in Elysian Park, Los Angeles, and a laundry mark on a towel wrapped round the legs led the police to an apartment house, where they interviewed a young man who gave his name as Evans. Not until some time later did the police realise that a shirt covering Marian Parker's trunk bore the same initials as the one worn by Evans when he was interviewed. The police returned to the apartment house, but the young man had disappeared. Fingerprints in the apartment established his true identity as Edward Hickman.

Captured in Seattle on 23 December, Hickman twice tried to commit suicide during the train journey to Los Angeles, but the sight of his name composed in headline type quite cured his depression. He revelled in his celebrity, chatting for hours on end with reporters and sob sisters, and flexing his facial muscles for the benefit of photographers, who generally respected his request for head-and-shoulder pictures that hid his lack of stature.

Soon after his arrest, Hickman stated that he had kidnapped Marian Parker because he needed $1,500 for college tuition. It seems more likely, however, that he considered the ransom money as a fringe benefit from the crime, and that the true motive was vengeance: he had recently completed a prison sentence for forgery while employed as a clerk at the same bank as the child's father, and it was established that he blamed Parker for the prosecution.

Awaiting trial, Hickman confided in a fellow prisoner that he intended to feign insanity, and described in some detail how he planned to do this. The prisoner informed the district attorney, who called him as a witness. Hickman was found guilty of the kidnapping and murder, and there was virtually no argument that he was legally sane: he had known what he was doing, and had known that what he was doing was wrong.

Hickman was hanged at San Quentin Prison. Considering the enormity and variety of his crimes against the Parker family, it was a small price to pay.

6 Rising Sun

No one would deny that—whether innocent as the jury at his trial decided, or guilty as most students of the case believe—Robert Wood certainly deserved to be hanged for the murder of Phyllis Dimmock in 1907.

He had as much luck in the final quarter of that year as many men, regarding themselves fortunate, accumulate in a decade or more. He was lucky in being represented by Arthur Newton, possibly the cleverest and almost certainly the most unscrupulous solicitor in criminal practice at that time; he was lucky in being defended at the trial by Sir Edward Marshall Hall, supremely eloquent and ingenious in a case that perfectly fitted his talents as a jury advocate. And, by one of the oddest paradoxes in social history, he had the great good fortune to have the falsity of his alibi revealed by the person upon whom it depended: to the public, and therefore to the jury, it seemed that he had been betrayed, Iscariot-fashion, for money, and this notion was perverted into an atmosphere of sympathy towards Wood, who became transmuted into the second victim of the case, far more worthy of pity than the wanton Phyllis Dimmock.

○○○○○

Her body was found by Bertram Shaw, the man with whom she had lived, ostensibly as his wife, for some nine months. Shaw was a dining-car chef on the Midland Railway; his working routine was to leave St Pancras Station for Sheffield in the afternoon, and to return the following morning on a train that arrived in London at about eleven. This arrangement suited Phyllis down to the ground, for it meant that while Shaw was away, she was able to supplement her housekeeping money by having male paying guests at the two-roomed flat in Camden Town which they rented for 8s (40p) a week. Shaw afterwards professed ignorance of Phyllis's extra-common-marital activities, but it is hard to believe that, even if he did not find out for himself, none of the neighbours in St Paul's Road apprised him of the nocturnal comings and goings at number twenty-nine, for Phyllis was a popular whore, and it was rare for her to spend a night alone.

On the hot and cloudless morning of Thursday, 12 September 1907, Shaw arrived home as usual, at 11.30. Receiving no reply when he knocked at the locked door of the first-floor flat, he obtained entry with a duplicate key borrowed from the landlady, who lived in the basement. The parlour was a shambles: every drawer had been ransacked and most of their contents strewn about the floor. There were four empty stout bottles and the remains of a meal on the table; places were set for two, indicating that Phyllis had entertained someone to supper. The folding doors to the bedroom were locked, and as there was no sign of the key and no answer to his frantic knocking, Shaw smashed them open. Rushing to the bed, he pulled aside the tumbled and blood-soaked sheets and blankets.

The naked body was lying in a position of sleep, and the face held the expression of a peaceful dream. The head, resting on a pillow, was almost completely severed; only the vertebrae had resisted the knife. Blood had seeped through the flock mattress and spilled on to the floor to form an obscene puddle that extended halfway across the room.

When he had recovered from the initial shock, Shaw made a hasty search of the flat and found that some pieces of jewellery and a purse were missing; yet on the chest of drawers, in plain view, were two gold rings. It seemed, therefore, either that Phyllis Dimmock had been murdered by an unobservant thief or that the missing articles had been taken only to simulate the motive of robbery.

One of the dead woman's most cherished possessions, a post-card album that had normally been kept on a small table in the parlour, was lying open on top of a sewing machine in the bed-room; a cursory examination showed that some cards had been torn out, and it occurred to Shaw—and later to the police—that the murderer had searched for, and taken, certain cards that connected him with his victim.

❍❍❍❍❍

From the degree of rigor mortis, the police surgeon estimated the time of death as between 4 and 6 o'clock in the morning. Neither the landlady nor her husband had heard any suspicious sounds. The landlady had last seen Phyllis Dimmock, with her hair in curlers, at about 7.30 in the evening, and had heard her leaving the house three-quarters of an hour later.

The police were at first unsuccessful in tracing her movements later that night. She had *not* visited the Rising Sun, a nearby public house that had been her favourite rendezvous and the market place for her trade. But several of the bar-room habitués mentioned to the police that they had seen her on more than one occasion recently with a 'rather strange young man'; statements from other witnesses, most of them members or entrepreneurs of the oldest profession, referred to the same young man and extended the period of his acquaintanceship with Phyllis Dimmock to fifteen months. The police distilled the various descriptions into the following:

> About 30 years of age. Height, 5 feet 7 inches. Sallow complexion. Dark hair. Clean shaven. Peculiar difference about eyes. He is a man of good education and of shabby-genteel appearance.

A further distinctive detail was added to this description when a man called Robert MacCowan came forward. According to his story, he had passed through St Paul's Road at about ten minutes to five on the morning of the murder; hearing footsteps behind him, he had turned to see a man leaving number twenty-nine and walking away in the opposite direction. MacCowan described him as a stiff-built man, 5ft 7 or 8in in height, wearing a bowler hat and a dark overcoat with the collar turned up. But what MacCowan remembered most vividly was the man's walk:

64

I noticed a peculiar jerk of the shoulders. .... His left hand was in his pocket, or down by his side, and he jerked the right shoulder forward as he walked.

Although the police were chiefly interested in tracing the ubiquitous young man of the witnesses' statements, they made every effort to identify other men who had been beguiled by Phyllis Dimmock, and it was from one of these, a ship's cook with the repetitious name of Robert Roberts, that they obtained several important clues. On the Sunday before the murder, Roberts had met Phyllis Dimmock in the bar of the Rising Sun, and after a short discussion on matters of finance they had left to spend the night together. Roberts, a truly satisfied customer, had returned to the flat on the following two nights, Monday and Tuesday, and, his virility and savings being sufficient, had suggested a further episode on the Wednesday, only to be told that an advance booking precluded such an arrangement. Before he had left the flat on the Wednesday morning, the post had arrived and the girl had shown him part of a letter, masking from his view the preceding sentences and a postscript that directly followed. He remembered the message as:

Dear Phillis, Will you meet me at the bar of the Eagle at Camden Town, 8.30 tonight, Wednesday.

Bert

Phyllis Dimmock had then taken a postcard from the chest of drawers and handed it to him to read. On one side was a picture of a woman embracing a child, and on the reverse side the address and the words:

Phillis Darling, If it pleases you meet me 8.15 p.m. at the [here was a cartoon drawing of a rising sun]. Yours to a cinder, Alice.

After replacing the card in the drawer (no doubt with the idea of pasting it into her album at some later date), Phyllis Dimmock had set fire to the letter and dropped it into the empty fire grate.

Roberts, who seems to have had a near-photographic memory, recalled that both the letter and the postcard were written in indelible lead; in his opinion, both were in the same hand.

The Rising Sun postcard

The police would no doubt have viewed parts of Roberts's story with some suspicion had it not been for two facts: first, he produced a water-tight alibi for the night of the crime, and second, in the fire grate they had already found the charred remains of a letter on which the following syllables were decipherable:

ill . . . you . . . aɪ of the . . . e . . . Town . . . Wednes
if . . . rest . . . excuse . . . good . . . fond . . . Mon . . . from . . . the

The first group of syllables provided perfect corroboration of Roberts's account of the letter received by Phyllis Dimmock, for they fitted exactly into the message he remembered:

Dear Phi*ll*is, Will *you* meet me at the b*ar of the* Eagle at
Camden *Town*, 8.30 tonight, *Wednes*day.

Bert

The police failed to find the 'rising sun' postcard, but it seems
that their search was not all that thorough. A few days later
Bertram Shaw decided to move from the flat to a single room in
the same house, and when he was emptying the chest of drawers,
he discovered the card tucked out of sight beneath a folded sheet
of newspaper that lined the bottom of one of the drawers.

Facsimiles of this postcard, and of three other cards with
similar handwriting that were found in the album, were circulated
to the press in the hope that their publication would lead to the
identification of the writing. Most national newspapers co-
operated by publishing one or other of the facsimiles together
with the formal request from the Commissioner of Police for
information; but on Sunday, 29 September, the *News of the
World* went one better than its competitors by reproducing the
'rising sun' postcard beneath the caption 'Can You Recognise
This Writing?' and offering £100 reward to anyone who could.

○─○─○─○─○

One of the millions of readers of the *News of the World* was a
girl called Ruby Young who described herself as an artist's model
but was in reality a member of the same profession as Phyllis
Dimmock. She recognised the handwriting on the postcard at
once; and not only the handwriting, but also the individual style
of the cartoon. They belonged, she felt sure, to a young man
whom she had known for about three years; the relationship,
professional at first, had gradually become one of mutual affection, even love on her part, but she had seen less of him in recent
months and was reconciled to his having discarded her for
another woman, or other women.

Ruby Young wrote a letter to the *News of the World*; but it was
never posted, for soon afterwards the young man turned up at her
flat in Earls Court. His name was Robert William Thomas
George Cavers Wood. He lived in the St Pancras district with his

67

father (who, if he bestowed as many names on his other children, must have found it hard to avoid duplication, for Robert had nineteen brothers and sisters). An artist-engraver—and a talented one whose work had been admired by William Morris—he had well-paid and secure employment with a firm of glass-makers in Gray's Inn Road. In his spare time, when he was not indulging

'Myself'—a sketch by Robert Wood

his *nostalgie de la boue* in the sawdust-speckled bars and dimly lit whores' havens of Camden Town and Islington, he did freelance cartoon drawing for a number of periodicals.

When Ruby Young showed him the letter that was waiting to be posted he admitted that the 'rising sun' postcard was in his handwriting. He had, he said, been in the bar of the Rising Sun on the evening of Friday, 6 September, when a young woman, a complete stranger, had asked him for a penny to put in the mechanical organ. They had got talking, and he had shown her some picture postcards that he happened to have with him, souvenirs of a holiday in Bruges. She had asked him to send her one after writing 'something nice' on it and, on the spur of the moment, he had composed a mock invitation, which she had told him to sign 'Alice', as otherwise 'the governor might cut up rough'. He had put the card in his pocket and, after buying her another drink, had said goodbye. The following day, quite by coincidence, he had met the woman in the street, and she had reminded him about the card; he had promised to post it, and had done so on the Sunday evening, afterwards thinking no more about it. On the Monday evening he had again visited the Rising Sun, and had again chatted with the woman and bought her a few drinks. He had not seen her since.

As Ruby Young listened to this story, she must have thought back to her last two meetings with Robert Wood. A week after the discovery of the murder in Camden Town, she had received a telegram from him, his first communication with her for more than a month:

Meet me at Phit-Eesi's tonight 6.30. Bob.

When she had met him outside Phit-Eesi's, which was a shoe shop in Southampton Row, he had said that he needed her help: 'If any questions are ever asked you by anyone, will you say that you always saw me on Monday and Wednesday nights?' He had given no reason for the unusual request, but she had consented.

Three days later, on Monday, 23 September, she had received a postcard from Wood which contained the message:

Sweetheart, If it is convenient for you, will you meet me as before at Phit-Eesi's, 6.30, and we will have tea together and then go to the theatre, which I hope will be a little ray of sunshine in your life. Goodbye. R.W.

69

They had gone to the Prince of Wales Theatre to see *Miss Hook of Holland*, and afterwards, waiting at a bus stop, Wood had suddenly said: 'Don't forget now—Mondays and Wednesdays.'

The reason for the meetings, for the repeated request, for Wood's visit that evening, was now clear, and Ruby Young was faced with a choice of evils: either she could post the letter or help to concoct a false alibi. She suggested that he should go to the police but he explained: 'I cannot prove where I was on the Wednesday night, that's why I can't go to them. I was out alone, walking, and no one was with me who could speak for me.' Once again he asked her to stick to the story about the Monday and Wednesday nights, and eventually she agreed.

'The best thing for me to do', she said, 'is to say that I met you at 6.30 at Phit-Eesi's, and we had tea at Lyons' Cafe, and then after tea we went down Kingsway to the Strand and straight on to Hyde Park Corner. Then we'd better say we walked along the park straight out to Brompton Oratory, and got there at half-past ten. We will say that we parted there: you went back by tube to King's Cross and got back home just before midnight.'

And that was how it was left.

Ruby Young would probably have had second thoughts if she had known that Wood had already enlisted the aid of others in avoiding any connection with the case. Only the day before, a man called Tinkham, a foreman at the glass works, had spoken to him about the postcard and he had admitted that the handwriting was his; he had told Tinkham the same story he told Ruby Young, and the foreman had agreed to say nothing about the card after Wood had told him that his father was suffering from gouty eczema, 'and if it came to his knowledge that I was in any way mixed up in the affair it might have dire results'.

A week before the discussion with Tinkham, Wood had called on his friend Joseph Lambert, a bookseller in Charing Cross Road, and had reminded him that at about 9 o'clock on the vital Wednesday evening they had met by chance in the bar of the Eagle, opposite Camden Town Station. Wood had been with a young woman whom he had introduced as 'Phyllis', and who had apologised for her hair being in curlers by saying: 'I hope you

will excuse me for being so untidy, as I have just run out.'
Lambert had had a drink with them, and had then left them
together in the bar. When Wood had called on Lambert on
20 September, he had said: 'I have seen Mr Moss, the head man
at the works, and he has been talking about the Camden Town
murder. If he says anything to you, will you tell him that we had
a drink, *but leave the girl out?*' Without asking for further
explanation, Lambert had agreed.

*The meeting at the Rising Sun, sketched by Robert Wood in
Brixton Prison*

Ruby Young saw Wood on two occasions after his Sunday
visit, and both times he reminded her of her promise. 'Yes, I'll
be true,' she replied abruptly. 'Don't bother me. It's getting on
my nerves.'

And it was; soon the secret became too much for her to bear
alone and she told a friend—in confidence, of course—of Wood's
dilemma. The friend passed the secret on to one of his own

friends, who happened to be a reporter, and in no time at all the secret was shared with Inspector Arthur Neil, the detective in charge of the investigations into the murder of Phyllis Dimmock.

At 6.30 on the evening of 4 October, as he was leaving work, Wood was met by Ruby Young, who shook hands with him. It was the signal to Neil, who made himself known to Wood and asked him to step into a waiting cab. 'Very well,' Wood said equably. 'You will allow me to wish my young lady goodbye before I go.' He then turned to Ruby Young and uttered a piece of solipsistic jingoism that must have sounded rather bizarre in the absence of a brass band accompaniment: 'Goodbye, dear. Don't worry. I have to go with these gentlemen. If England wants me, she must have me. Don't cry, but be true.'

During the drive to Highgate Police Station, Wood insisted that he had made no secret of having written the 'rising sun' postcard. After being cautioned, he told Neil: 'My young brother, or my step-brother, called my attention to the handwriting of the postcard when it came out in the Sunday paper. I told them it was *like* my handwriting, but I knew at the same time that I wrote the card, and the same night I had a chat with my brother Charles, a conscientious sort of chap who lives at Museum Street, and his wife Bessie. I was advised to go to Scotland Yard. But about that time I was very busy at the office with the work of the chief, who was away on holiday at the time. My brother then said that the next best thing to do was to write a letter, addressed to one of us, care of the poste restante at the G.P.O. We sent the letter, addressed to Charles, and it stated that I acknowledged writing the postcard, and giving my reasons for not coming forward. Now I want you to get that letter, inspector, because it shows that I did not conceal the matter.'

What Wood meant by this is anyone's guess; the surprising thing is that not only he, but also his brother and his brother's wife, considered that by writing a letter confessing a secret—a letter that was to be opened only in the event of the secret's being discovered—all secrecy was erased. The letter, signed by Charles Carlyle Wood, Bessie M. Wood and Robert Wood, was later obtained by the police from the poste restante department at St Martin's le Grand Post Office. It read as follows:

43 Museum Street,
London, W.C.,
Sunday, Sept. 29, '07

We, the undersigned, make this statement and place it in the charge of the poste restante at St. Martin's le Grand in order to safeguard our good faith in the matter should our course of action be impeached. We, the first two signatories, are aware from his own full avowal that the post card published in the newspapers of September 27th and 28th by desire of the police in order to obtain information in the Camden Town murder case is in the handwriting of, and was written by, Robert Wood, of 12 Frederick Street. We jointly are anxious to help the police in every way possible; but we are also anxious to avoid the publicity and personal trouble occasioned by an immediate communication.

Having regard to the non-reliability of newspaper reports, theories, and comments, and being quite satisfied of Robert Wood's *bona fides* and that his contribution to the matter can aid but little, we consider it wise to await the results produced at the adjourned inquest on September 29th [a mistake: the inquest was resumed on the 30th], and while trusting that the intervention of Robert Wood may thereby be unnecessary, at the same time we determine, should no satisfaction arise from the inquest, to make the avowal of Robert Wood without delay.

This last paragraph, although high-sounding, was actually only a legalistic form of words, a clause that could be conveniently forgotten but that for the time being salved the consciences of Charles and Bessie Wood. Not only was the resumed inquest of 30 September adjourned days before Wood's arrest, but Wood himself admitted that the letter 'was intended to be opened in the event of the police calling on me for an explanation'.

At the station Wood dictated a statement in which he repeated the story he had told Ruby Young and Tinkham about the three casual meetings with Phyllis Dimmock. And, quite convinced that Ruby Young would 'be true', he recited the false alibi for the night of the crime.

Two identification parades were held, and Wood was picked out by several witnesses, most of them prostitutes who claimed to have seen him with Phyllis Dimmock during the past fifteen

73

months. He was also identified as having been with the woman in the bar of the Eagle on the Wednesday night. The most unorthodox identification was that of Robert MacCowan (he who claimed to have seen a man leaving 29 St Paul's Road on the morning of the murder); he was unable to pick out anyone at the parade, but as soon as the men started to move away, he identified Wood by his walk.

O-O-O-O-O

Wood was charged with the murder, and almost at once his luck changed, not merely for the better, but for the best. His employers subscribed £1,000 to a defence fund, thus enabling his solicitor, Arthur Newton, to spend lavishly in scheming an answer to the prosecution case and to brief Marshall Hall to lead three junior counsel at the trial.

In the period between the committal proceedings and the trial, public sympathy for Wood came close to mass hysteria. Engendered by the belief that he had been betrayed for money by a prostitute, the sympathy was artfully nurtured by Newton who, when cross-examining at the police court, implied that the testimony of the other prostitutes and of MacCowan, who was unemployed, had been purchased by the police.

Ruby Young had to go into hiding and many of the other prosecution witnesses received threats. MacCowan stated: 'I might have committed the murder myself. Letters have been sent to me threatening to cut my throat, "blood money" has been chalked over my door, and my children were even told of it at the county council school where they attend. In future, even if I actually saw with my own eyes a man getting his throat cut in the street, I do not think I would give evidence again.'

O-O-O-O-O

Wood's demeanour at the trial, which began at the Old Bailey on 12 December, was that of a rather bored spectator. He whiled away much of the time by drawing sketches and caricatures of the

'A game of cards'—Wood's view of the fight for his life

lawyers and of the stage celebrities who filled the seats reserved
for distinguished visitors.

At the end of the first day, back in his cell at Brixton Prison,
he wrote to his brother:

Dear Charles,
I am just back. So sorry I could not grasp you by the hand
today.
I commenced a letter yesterday to Bessie, but it is bundled
away among my things.
Of course I have nothing now of my possessions except the
things I stand in.
My feelings were strange today. Such that I cannot describe
though quite peaceful. Whispers of good cheer came from
every direction and even the orderly that tends my room moved
silently and with some reverence this morning.
Little did I think that one day I should appear on the capital

charge under that beautiful gold figure of Justice (by
Frampton, R. A.) that towers above the Old Bailey—I think
you have admired it.
I have a memory of sitting with this great sculptor at supper on
more than one occasion.
I liked Marshall Hall's manner when he spoke to me today,
and he is apparently a splendid man.
I am rather cut off now from Mr Newton so please call his
attention to any point; though I expect they view things
differently from us. I mean the legal mind.
Pardon, dear Charlie, if I have omitted any due remarks or
thanks.
To be tried for one's life is I think sufficient for the day and I
am now weary.
I must ask you all to be of good cheer and to take good care of
yourselves.
I understand that there are great odds to face that may end
disastrously; but I will carry my head high for I have done no
grievous wrong.
Goodbye, with fondest wishes to all.

Bob

Marshall Hall's defence of Wood was a sort of forensic con-
juring act; several of his tricks were patently obvious and one
or two went wrong, but this didn't really matter because the
members of the jury were on his side from the beginning, ready
to forgive and forget any mistakes and naiveties in the defence
case.

Wood stuck to his story that he had first met Phyllis Dimmock
on the Friday before she was murdered, so in dealing with the
prostitutes who claimed that the acquaintanceship was of far
longer duration, Marshall Hall sought more to discredit their
characters than to challenge their evidence. Cross-examining
Bertram Shaw and Robert Roberts, he implied that *even* if the
jury accepted their water-tight alibis, their evidence lacked credi-
bility because, as suspects, they had had every reason to lie to the
police in order to exculpate themselves.

Marshall Hall's most spectacular success was in seeming to
demolish the evidence of Robert MacCowan, whose poor showing

*Robert Wood sketching by the light of a gas jet outside his cell.
The sketch on the floor is of Sir Hall Caine, one of the celebrities
who attended the trial*

in the witness box is exemplified by the following extract from his cross-examination:

What sort of morning was it [just before 5am on 12 September]?
It was a drizzly, thick, muggy morning.
Do you know that not a drop of rain fell in London that day?
I call weather like that, when there is dew, 'muggy'. I have not swallowed the dictionary. I am Suffolk. That is how we talk in Suffolk.
In Suffolk a morning not raining is drizzly?
Yes.
What kind of a morning was it?
It was a foggy morning.
You have described it before as a drizzly, thick, foggy, muggy morning, getting daylight, but not yet daylight?
Yes. . . .
Have you no regard for human life?
Yes, or I should not have come forward and given evidence. One life is as good as another.
Is that how you behave in Suffolk?
Yes.

The defence cast further doubt on MacCowan's powers of observation by calling as one of their witnesses a member of the electricity department of St Pancras Borough Council. Mac-Cowan asserted that when he passed through St Paul's Road at about 4.50 on the morning of the murder, the street lamps had still been alight; according to the electrician, however, the lamps had been turned out ten minutes before. This point was more showy than valid, for it is unlikely that MacCowan's cheap alarm clock kept perfect time, or that his estimate of how long it took him to walk from his home to St Paul's Road was accurate to the minute. At all events, neither this point nor any of the others made by the defence explained away MacCowan's identification of Wood by his walk, the peculiarity of which was referred to by other witnesses.

The importance of the charred letter, which proved that a definite appointment had been made, was played down by the defence. In the witness box Wood admitted that the handwriting

'Lady Diabolo of Monte Carlo'—sketched by Robert Wood
while awaiting trial

was his, but maintained that the words were not part of a letter. As if this assertion were not ludicrous enough, he suggested that the words were 'fragments of some amusing phrases and sketches' that Phyllis Dimmock had taken from him during one of their meetings at the Rising Sun: 'She had many little things I had written. She looked through my letters and papers which I used to take out of my pocket in pulling out my sketch-book in the bar. Girls like that are very bold. . . . When I pulled out my sketch-book everything fell out. She was very forward. It may

Ruby Young—sketched from the dock by Robert Wood

have been written in her presence or it may have been in my pocket. I lay stress on the "may have been". I sent no message to her. . . . I cannot imagine [the object of] a careless scribble like that.'

⊙⊙⊙⊙⊙

The jury retired at 7.45 on the evening of the sixth day of the trial. They returned a quarter of an hour later, and Robert Wood earned a place in legal history by being the first defendant in a murder case to be found not guilty after giving evidence on his own behalf. He listened to the verdict calmly, with a slight smile, and before being discharged, tidied up a sketch he had made of Mr Justice Grantham during the summing-up.

The cheers in court that greeted the verdict were taken up by the crowd that thronged the streets around the Old Bailey, and a 'vast cordon' of police was needed to escort Wood and his many relatives to a restaurant in the Strand, where his father made a speech of thanks from the balcony.

Theatrical performances were interrupted to announce the news, and at His Majesty's Mrs Beerbohm Tree earned the greatest applause of her career by rushing on to the stage and gasping: 'I have just arrived from the court—the court where young Robert Wood stood in peril of his life. I am glad to be able to tell you that the jury found him not guilty.'

By eleven o'clock the crowd outside the Old Bailey had dwindled slightly, but only to become a mob, and Ruby Young, the girl who contributed almost as much to Robert Wood's acquittal as to his arrest, had to be smuggled out of the building disguised as a charwoman.

7 Sacco-Vanzetti

Millions of words have been written, millions more spoken, about the case of the Italian-born anarchists, Nicola Sacco, a shoemaker, and Bartolomeo Vanzetti, a fish peddler, who in 1921 were found guilty of murdering two men during a payroll robbery at South Braintree, Massachusetts. Unfortunately, most of these words have come from radicals, from people who see Sacco and Vanzetti as symbols of capitalist injustice, latterday crucifix figures, rather than as defendants in a murder case. When radicalism is the motive for presenting an account of a criminal case the result is almost invariably as perverted as the most reactionary propaganda.

Undeniably, there were defects in the legal process that, eight years after their indictment, took Sacco and Vanzetti to the electric chair at Charlestown Prison; undeniably, too, their anarchist activities did not endear them to certain Massachusetts lawyers and politicians (Webster Thayer, the trial judge, is said to have remarked to a friend at a football game: 'Did you see what I did with those anarchistic bastards the other day?'). But it is nonsense to suggest—as so many commentators on the case have done—that a list of symptoms of prejudice amounts to the conclusion that Sacco and Vanzetti were victims of a miscarriage of justice; that, simply because they were anarchists, they were convicted of a crime they did not commit. By a similar method of reasoning one could make a martyr of Adolf Hitler.

The evidence—or rather, what one can discern of the evidence through the verbiage of implication and deduction from half-stated facts—indicates that Sacco was guilty but that the case against Vanzetti was less conclusive, perhaps unproven.

ooooo

At the beginning of their imprisonment, while their lawyers were collecting affidavits and arguing motions for retrial and while left-wing individuals and organisations were turning the case into a cause, Sacco and Vanzetti studied English under the tutorage of women members of the New England Civil Liberties Committee so as to be able to read revolutionary works and to express their beliefs. In some of the letters they wrote in English —those of Vanzetti particularly—they achieved a rare, at times poetic, eloquence; but more often it was a soapbox eloquence, the eloquence of a manifesto. One gets the feeling that many of the letters were written to specifications prescribed by others— that they were written in the knowledge that they would be edited and typed on stencils to be duplicated and sent to press agencies.

Vanzetti's first letter in English was written at the end of June 1921. It was to a well-wisher:

I was just thinging what I would do for past the long days jail. I was saying to mysefl: Do some work. But what? Write. A gentle motherly figure came to my mind and I rehear the voice: Why don't you write something now? It will be useful to you now when you will be free. Just at that time I received your letter.
Tank to you from the bottom of my earth for your confidence in my innocence; I am so. I did not splittel a drop of blood, or still a cent in all my life. A little knowledge of the past; a sorrowful experience of the life itself had given to me some ideas very different from those of many other umane beings. But I wish to convince my fellow men that only with virtue and honesty is possible for us to find a little happyness in this world. I preached; I worked. I wished with all my faculties that the social whealth should belong to every umane creatures, so well as it was the fruit of the work of all. But this do not mean robbery for insurrection.

Soon afterwards, writing to the same person, his style was almost Whitman-like as he expressed his longing for freedom:

O the blissing green of the wilderness and of the open land—O the blue vastness of the Oceans—the fragrances of the flowers and the sweetness of the fruits—The sky reflecting lakes—the singing turrents—the telling brooks—O the valleys, the hills—the awful Alps! O the mistic dawn—the roses of the Aurora, the glory of the moon—O the sunset—the twilight—O the supreme extasies and mistery of the starry nights, heavenly creatures of the eternity.

Yes, Yes, all this is real actuallity but not to us, not to us chained—and just and simple because we, being chained, have not the freedom to use our natural faculty of locomotion to carry us from our cells to the open orizon—under the Sun at daytime—under the visible stars, at night.

As the years passed, and as the number of stratagems for postponing the executions diminished, Vanzetti's letters became almost wholly concerned either with defining the anarchist's creed or with attacking Judge Thayer and other 'State tools and murderors'. But in a letter written in December 1926 he thought back to his childhood in Italy, and described his father's garden at Villafalletto:

It takes a poet of first magnitude to worthly speak of it, so beautiful, unspeakably beautiful it is . . . the singing birds there; black merles of the golden bick, and ever more golden troath; the golden oriols, the gold-finches, the green finches, the chaf-finches, the neck-crooking, the green ficks; the unmachable nightingales, the nightingales over-all. Yet, I think that the wonder of my garden's wonders is the banks of its path. Hundreds of grass, leaves of wild flowors witness there the almighty genios of the universal architecture—reflecting the sky, the Sun, the moon, the stars, all of its lights and colors. The forgetmenot are nations there, and nation are the wild daisies.

❍❍❍❍❍

At last, in August 1927, all legal means of postponing the executions were exhausted; Sacco and Vanzetti were told that they were to die at midnight on Monday the 22nd. The day before, Sacco completed a farewell letter to his thirteen-year-old

son Dante. He had planned to have its contents kept secret for
five years, but he agreed to release it when told that it might
influence the state governor to commute the sentences. The
following is the edited version:

Much have we suffered during this long Calvary. We protest
today as we protested yesterday. We protest always for our
freedom.
If I stopped hunger strike the other day, it was because there
was no more sign of life in me. Because I protested with my
hunger strike yesterday as today I protest for life and not for
death.
I sacrificed because I wanted to come back to the embrace of
your dear little sister Ines [born after Sacco's arrest] and your
mother and all the beloved friends and comrades of life and not
death. So Son, today life begins to revive slow and calm, but
yet without horizon and always with sadness and visions of
death. . . .
But remember always, Dante, in the play of happiness, don't
you use all for yourself only, but down yourself just one step,
at your side and help the weak ones that cry for help, help the
prosecuted and the victim, because that are your better
friends; they are the comrades that fight and fall as your
father and Bartolo fought and fell yesterday for the conquest of
the joy of freedom for all and the poor workers. In this
struggle of life you will find more love and you will be
loved. . . .
Much have I thought of you when I was lying in the death
house—the singing, the kind tender voices of the children from
the playground, where there was all the life and the joy of
liberty—just one step from the wall which contains the buried
agony of three buried souls [a third man was to be executed on
the 22nd]. It would remind me so often of you and your sister
Ines, and I wish I could see you every moment. But I feel
better that you did not come to the death-house so that you
could not see the horrible picture of three lying in agony
waiting to be electrocuted, because I do not know what effect
it would have on your young age. . . .
Dante, I say once more to love and be nearest to your mother
and the beloved ones in these sad days, and I am sure that
with your brave heart and kind goodness they will feel less

discomfort. And you will also not forget to love me a little for I do—O, Sonny! thinking so much and so often of you.
Best fraternal greetings to all the beloved ones, love and kisses to your little Ines and mother. Most hearty affectionate embrace.

Vanzetti, a bachelor, also wrote a farewell letter to Dante Sacco:

I still hope, and we will fight until the last moment, to rivendicate our right to live and be free, but all the forces of the State and of the Money and reaction are deadly against us because we are libertarian or anarchist.
I write little of this because you are now a yet to little-boy to understand this things and other things of which I would like to reason with you.
But if you do well, you will grow and understand your father's and my case and your father's and my principles, for which we shall soon be put to death.
I tell you that for and of all I know of your father, he is not a criminal, but one of the bravest men I ever knew. One day you will understand what I am about to tell you: That your father has sacrificed everything dear and sacred to the human heart and soul for his fate in liberty and justice for all. That day you will be proud of your father; and if you come brave enough, you will take his place in the struggle between tyranny and liberty and you will vindicate his (our) names and our blood.
If we have to die now, you shall know, when you will be able to understand this tragedy in its fullness, how good and brave your mother has been with you, your father and I, during these eight years of struggle, sorrow, passion, anguish and agony.
Even from now you shall be good, brave with your mother, with Ines, and with Suzy [Susie Valdinoce, the sister of an anarchist killed in a bomb explosion]—brave, good Suzy—and do all you can to console and help them.
I would like you will also remember me as a comrade and friend of your father, your mother, Ines, Suzy and you, and I secure you that neither I have been a criminal, that I have committed no robbery and no murder, but only fought modestly to abolish crimes from among mankind and for the

liberty of all.

Remember Dante, each one who will say otherwise of your father and I, is a lier, insulting innocent death men who have been brave in their life.

Remember and know also, Dante, that if your father and I would have been hypocrits and rinnegetors of our faith, we would have not have been put to death. They would not even have convicted a lebbrous dogs; not even executed a deadly poisoned scorpion on such evidence as that they framed against us. They would have given a new trial to a matricide and abitual felon on the evidence we presented for a new trial. Remember, Dante, remember always these things; we are not criminals; they convicted us on a frame-up; they denied us a new trial; and if we will be executed after seven years, four months and 17 days of unspeakable tortures and wrongs, it is for what I have already told you; because we were for the poor and against the exploitation and oppression of the man by the man.

The documents of our case, which you and other ones will collect and preserve, will proof you that your father, your mother, yourself, Inez, I and my family are sacrificed by and to a State Reason of the American Plutocratic reaction.

The day will come when you will understand the atrocious sense of the above-written words, in all its fullness. Then you will honor us.

Now Dante, be brave and good always. I embrace you.

ooooo

Despite a last-minute flurry of appeals, the executions took place as scheduled. The two men met their deaths with a pathetic dignity. Sacco was the first to die. 'Farewell!' he shouted as the signal was given for the switch to be pulled, and then in Italian: 'Mother!'

As soon as Sacco's body had been removed, Vanzetti was escorted into the execution chamber. He paused just inside the door and, addressing himself to the prison warden, said firmly:

'I wish to say to you that I am innocent. I have never done a crime—some sins, but never any crime. I thank you for everything you have done for me. I am innocent of all crime, not only this one, but of all, of all. I am an innocent man.'

He was strapped to the chair, his eyes covered, as he spoke his last words:

'I now wish to forgive some people for what they are doing to me.'

8 Red Barn

In the several plays and ballads inspired by the murder in the Red Barn at Polstead, Maria Marten is portrayed as the pure, simple daughter of a Suffolk mole-catcher. Actually, to paraphrase Wilde's idea of truth, Maria was rarely simple and, from the age of sixteen, never pure.

She had at least three illegitimate children. The father of the first child, which was born in the spring of 1820 and lived only a few weeks, was Thomas Corder, the eldest son of a well-to-do local farmer. A year later, when Maria was twenty-one, she gave birth to a son by Peter Matthews, the rakish brother of the owner of Polstead Hall; this child, Thomas Henry, survived, and Matthews paid the Martens £5 a quarter towards its support. In 1826 Maria conceived a child by twenty-three-year-old William Corder, the younger brother of Thomas; the child died—perhaps unnaturally—within two months and was secretly buried in a field at nearby Sudbury.

According to a contemporary description:

William Corder was five feet, four inches in height, and of slender make, and had a remarkable inclination to stoop forward in his walk, and held the lappel or breast of his coat in his left hand, when doing so. His complexion was fair, but not sickly; his face much freckled, and his eyes extremely weak, so much so, that he was often obliged to put a book very near them, in order to read its contents. . . . This young man appears to have indulged an ungovernable propensity for forming intimate connexions with females, notwithstanding which he was, in general, extremely cautious in his amours, in order to prevent discoveries. When the secret was disclosed, he used to boast of the favours with which he had been indulged, with a criminal flippancy.

After the death of the baby, Corder and Maria quarrelled frequently—chiefly, it seems, over Peter Matthews's most recent quarterly payment, which Maria (with good reason) accused Corder of stealing. Her father, apparently feeling that an unhappy marriage was better than no marriage at all, repeatedly reminded Corder of his promise to make Maria his wife; but Corder always either evaded the issue or named a date for the wedding and then concocted a reason for postponing it.

Maria Marten

On 18 May 1827, a Friday, Corder arrived at the Martens' cottage and announced that he was taking Maria to Ipswich for their marriage. 'The reason I go to Ipswich,' he said, 'is because John Baalham, the constable, came to me in the stable this morning, and told me he had a letter from a Mr Whitmore in

London, to proceed against Maria about her bastard children.'
He persuaded Maria to pack her clothes and disguise herself as
a man, and they set off for the Red Barn, where—so Corder
said—Maria was to change into her own clothes for the trip to
Ipswich. She was never seen alive again.

William Corder

The following Sunday, Corder again called at the Martens'
cottage. He and Maria were not yet married, he said, because the
licence had had to be sent to London for signature; he told Anne
Marten, the step-mother, that Maria was staying at Ipswich with
the sister of a friend of his. The reason for his 'returning' to
Polstead was that all his brothers were now dead and his widowed

mother needed his help in dealing with family business. The weeks passed, and Corder told different stories to different people to account for Maria's absence and to explain why no letters were received from her.

Apart from her family, the person most anxious to obtain news of her was Peter Matthews, who seems to have believed that if she was married he would no longer need to subsidise Thomas Henry. On 26 August Corder wrote to him:

Sir,
In reply to your generous letter which reached me yesterday, I beg to inform you that I was indeed innocent of Maria Marten's residence at the time you requested me to forward the letter I took from Bramford, and will candidly confess that Maria had been with a distant female relation of mine since the month of May. About five weeks ago they both went into Norfolk to visit some of my friends. On Friday week I received a letter from my kindred, who informed me that Maria was somewhat indisposed, and that they were then in a village called Herlingly, near Yarmouth.
I received an answer by the next post and enclosed your letter for Maria, which I found reached her perfectly safely, as I took the Yarmouth coach last Wednesday from Ipswich Lamb-Fair, and went to Herlingly, when I was sorry to learn that Maria's indisposition was occasioned by a sore gathering on the back of her hand, which caused her great pain, and which prevented her from writing to you, as her fingers are at present immovable.
Knowing you would be anxious to hear from her, I particularly wished her to write the first moment she found herself able, which she promised very faithfully to do. I gave her a particular account of our dialogue at Polstead Hall, not forgetting the remarkable kindness I received from you, which I shall ever most gratefully acknowledge. . . .
I remain, Sir,
Your most humble and obedient servant,
William Corder

Corder finally left Polstead for London on 18 September, exactly four months after Maria's disappearance. Confident, ap-

parently, that he could continue the deception indefinitely, he
made no attempt to hide his whereabouts, and a month later
wrote to Maria's father with the news that the marriage had
taken place:

> The Bull Inn,
> Leadenhall Street,
> London
> Thursday, 18th Oct.

Thomas Marten:
I am just arrived at London upon business respecting our
family affairs, and am writing to you before I take any
refreshment, because I should be in time for this night's post,
as my stay in town will be very short—anxious to return again
to her who is now my wife, and with whom I shall be one of
the happiest of men.

I should have had her with me, but it was her wish to stay at
our lodging at Newport, in the Isle of Wight, which she
described to you in her letter, and we were astonished that you
have not yet answered it, thinking illness must have been the
cause. In that she gave you a full description of our marriage,
and that Mr Rowland was 'daddy', and Miss Rowland
bridesmaid. Likewise told you that they came with us as far as
London, where we continued together very comfortable for
three days, when we parted with the greatest respect. Maria
and myself went on to the Isle of Wight, and they both
returned home.

I told Maria I should write to you directly I reached London,
who is very anxious to hear from you, fearful lest some strange
reason is the cause of your not writing. She requested that you
would inclose Mr Peter's [Matthews] letters in one of your
own, should he write to you, that we may know better how to
act. She is now mine, and I should wish to study for her
comfort, as well as my own. Maria desired me to give her love
to Nancy [Maria's sister], and a kiss for her little boy, hoping
that every care is taken of him; and tell your wife to let Nancy
have any of Maria's clothes she thinks proper for she says she
has got so many they will only spoil, and make use of any she
may like herself.

In her letter she said a great deal about little Henry, who she
feels anxious to hear about, and will take him to herself as soon

as we can get a farm whereby we can gain a livelihood, which I shall do the first I can meet with worth notice; for living without business is very expensive; still provisions are very reasonable in the Isle of Wight, I think cheaper than any part of England.

Thank God we are both well, hoping it will find you all the same. We have been a good deal on the water, and have had some seasickness, which I consider to have been very useful to us both—my cough I have lost entirely, which is a great consolation; in real truth, I feel better than I ever did before in my life, only in this short time. Maria told you, in her letter, how ill I was for two days, at Portsmouth, which is seven miles over the sea to the Isle of Wight, making altogether one hundred and thirty-nine miles from Polstead.

I would say more, but time will not permit; therefore, Maria unites with me for your welfare, and may every blessing attend you. Mind you direct for W.M.C. at the Bull Inn, Leadenhall Street, London. Write tomorrow if you can; if not, write soon enough for Saturday's post, that I may get it on Sunday morning, when I shall return to Maria directly I receive it. Inclose Mr Peter's letters and let us know whether he has acknowledged little Henry. You must try and read my scribble, but I fear you will never make it out.

I remain your well-wisher,
                                            W.C.

I think you had better burn all letters, after taking all directions, that nobody may form the least idea of our residence. Adieu.

Thomas Marten replied at once, and on Monday, 23 October, Corder wrote:

I received your letter this morning, which reached London yesterday, but letters are not delivered out here on a Sunday: that I discovered on making inquiry yesterday. However, I could not get through my business before this afternoon, and I am going to Portsmouth by this night's coach. I have this day been to the General Post Office, making inquiries about the letter Maria wrote to you on the 30th of September, which you say never came into your hands. The clerk of the Office traced the books back to the day it was wrote and he said a letter, directed as I told him to you, never came through their office, which I think is very strange. However, I am determined to find out how it was lost, if possible, but I must think coming over the water to Portsmouth, which I will inquire about tomorrow, when I hope to find out the mystery.

It is, I think, very odd that letters should be lost in this strange way. Was it not for the discovery of our residence, I would certainly indict the Post Office, but I cannot do that without making our appearance at a court-martial, which would be very unpleasant for us both. You wish for us to come to Polstead, which we should be very happy to do, but you are not aware of the danger. You may depend, if ever we fall into Mr P——'s hands, the consequences would prove fatal; therefore, should he write to you, or should he come to Polstead, you must tell him you have not the least knowledge of us, but you think we are gone into some foreign part. I think, if you don't hear from him before long, you had better write and tell him you cannot support the child without some assistance for we are gone you know not where.

If you tell him you hear from us, he will force you to say where we was, therefore I think it best not to acknowledge anything at all. I enclose £1, and you shall hear from us again in a short time. This will not reach you before Wednesday morning, as I am too late for this night's post. You said your wife did not like to take any of Maria's clothes; she said in her last letter, that her old clothes were at their service—I mean your wife and Nancy; but she shall write again as soon as possible. I must now bid you adieu. The coach will start in about ten minutes. I have been so much employed all this day that I could not write before. Believe me to be your well-wisher for your future welfare,

W.M.C.

The correspondence between Corder and Thomas Marten makes it clear that Matthews had decided to discontinue the payments towards the upkeep of Thomas Henry; the risk of his trying to trace Corder and Maria was no doubt magnified by Corder into an ideal excuse for staying away from Polstead and for not revealing the address in the Isle of Wight (a place which, as Corder took such pains to point out, was 139 miles from Polstead, just about as far south as it was possible to go without leaving the country; to Marten and his wife, neither of whom had ventured more than a few miles from their village, the island must have seemed as remote as the Indies).

Corder remained at the Bull for a further week, and would probably have stayed longer had he not met a prostitute who knew of his connection with Polstead. Fearing that she might inform the Martens of the meeting, he hurried away to the small coastal town of Seaford in Sussex.

○○○○○

Corder returned to London in November. Having gone to extreme lengths to prevent one marriage, he now went out of his way to arrange another, inserting the following advertisement in the *Morning Herald* of 12 November and the *Sunday Times* of the 25th:

MATRIMONY. A private gentleman, aged 24, entirely independent, whose disposition is not to be exceeded, has lately lost the chief of his family by the hand of Providence, which has occasioned discord among the remainder, under circumstances most disagreeable to relate. To any female of respectability who would study for domestic comfort, and willing to confide her future happiness in one every way qualified to render the marriage state desirable; as the advertiser is in affluence, the lady must have the power of some property, which may remain in her own possession. Many very happy marriages have taken place through means similar to this now resorted to, and it is hoped no one will answer this through impertinent curiosity; but should this meet the eye of any agreeable lady, who feels desirous of meeting with a sociable, tender, kind and sympathising companion, she will find this advertisement worthy of notice. Honour and secrecy may be relied on. As some security against idle applications, it is requested that letters may be addressed to A-Z, care of Mr Foster, stationer, No 68 Leadenhall Street, which will meet with the most respectful attention.

The advertisement brought ninety-nine replies. The first forty-five were handed over to Corder in one batch, and he never bothered to collect the rest. Such a large response can probably be ascribed to the sheer length of the advertisement; this, as well as making the advertisement more eye-catching, indicated that 'A-Z' was better off, or perhaps more open-handed, than most matrimonial advertisers, who condensed their conjugal desire into a couple of lines.

Matrimonial advertisements were almost as much a feature of the newspapers of the 1820s as are used car advertisements in the newspapers of today; even so, they were considered 'not quite nice'. It was a minor social sin for a woman who did not work for a living to be seen glancing at the matrimonial columns, and the idea of actually replying to an advertisement was tinged with scarlet. Many of the women who replied to Corder's advertisement used up sheets of notepaper in explaining how they had 'inadvertently', 'accidentally', or 'by the merest chance' happened to notice the word MATRIMONY; how, despite themselves, they had been forced to read on; and how, after considerable mental anguish, they had allowed their womanly feelings to overcome the guilt and embarrassment of communicating with 'A-Z'. Several replies claimed to be from go-betweens but were patently from excessively shy principals; there was no mistaking the true go-between letter, the most blatant of which came from a father offering his daughter's hand, sight of prospective husband unseen —'you can call here at any hour and take her away'. Few of the letters were as brief, open, and to the point as the first in the following selection:

Sir,
I have taken the earliest opportunity of addressing you with these few lines. According to your advertisement, as you being the age that will suit me, twenty-four and I am eighteen, so I think Providence as ordained that you and I shood come together, for I am not very pleacntury situated myself, and it appears that you are not. I am of very cheerful disposition, and shood study everything for your comfort and happiness. If it will suit you, the most convenient time to see me will be at

eleven o'clock in the morning, and three in the afternoon. If I
do not see you in a day or two, I shall think that you are
suited.
Till then, adieu.

Another letter, a small masterpiece of emphatic gentility,
began:

When a female breaks through the rules of eitiquette justly
prescribed for her sex, as a boundary which she must not pass
without sacrificing some portion of that delicacy which ought
to be her chief characteristic, it must be for some very urgent
reason, such as a *romantic* love, or a circumstance like the
present; and in answering your advertisement, I feel that I am,
in some degree, transgressing the law alluded to, and yet the
novelty and sentiments of the advertisement itself, so entirely
different from the language generally made use of (and which
alone induced me to answer it), almost assure me that no
improper advantage will be taken of the confidence I place in
the honour of the writer: however, as you request that no
person will write from motives of curiosity, I trust that no
feeling of that nature actuated you in giving me this
opportunity; but enough of preface.

Several timid pages later, the writer at last braced herself and
came to the point:

From the tenor of your advertisement, I presume fortune is
but a secondary consideration; a companion only is wanted
who would sympathise in all your joys or griefs, one who
would return kindness with kindness, love for love, and, as I
perfectly know my own heart, as far as regards those qualities,
I do not flatter myself when I say that such a companion would
I prove; and where confidence was shown, the fullest would be
returned. Pardon the warmth of my expressions, nor think me
forward in offering them, as I am no giddy girl: nor am I a
romantic old maid, but a warm-hearted affectionate girl, whose
age qualifies her to pass between the two characters, being just
turned twenty-one.

In contrast, another of the replies displayed a daunting confidence:

> If you really are inclined to marry, and all is true which you
> state, I think I am the person. My age is twenty-two, and am
> happy to say possess a most amiable disposition; can play the
> piano-forte and sing tolerably well; also other accomplishments
> which I think not worthy of statement. I have always been
> brought up domesticated, and am quite able to manage, let my
> situation be what it may; my wish is to settle in life, provided I
> meet with one who I think deserves such a wife as I shall
> make. . . .
> P.S. I have no fortune till the death of my mother.

Although a number of the women claimed to have fallen on
hard times, only one explained the circumstances of her fall:

> I have moved in society perhaps not inferior to the rank you
> hold; but, by a deviation from rectitude, which was occasioned
> by the too easily listening to the flattery of one whose vows I
> foolishly believed to be true, I am entirely deserted by my
> family, and banished from society; nevertheless, I flatter
> myself that I do not altogether merit such a fate, for I do
> assure you that no one could have acted more prudently than I
> have done since the unfortunate circumstance happened, which
> has very much destroyed my peace of mind; but I still hope to
> see better days.
> I am two-and-twenty years of age, but have not the least
> pretension to beauty—quite the contrary. I have a sweet little
> girl, who is my greatest comfort; she is sixteen months old, and
> is beginning to prattle very prettily; I have no fortune
> whatever, but am supporting myself by needle-work at
> present, until I can meet with something more to my
> advantage. I mention these facts that you may not be led into
> any error; for I should be extremely sorry to act with any
> duplicity towards any one, and I leave you to consider how far
> your generosity will extend to appreciate my wrongs, and
> excuse my past misconduct.

Corder's motive in advertising for a wife is by no means clear.

During his short stay at Seaford he had met a shy, slightly deaf young woman called Mary Moore who was on holiday there; her home was in Gray's Inn Terrace, London, where she lived with her mother and brother, and ran a school for young children. Corder and Mary Moore did not exchange addresses and, as far as is known, made no arrangement to continue the friendship—yet a week or so later they met again in a pastrycook's shop in Fleet Street. Perhaps this first London meeting was a coincidence. But it can hardly have been a coincidence that Mary Moore answered the 'A-Z' advertisement in the *Morning Herald*. Within a week of Corder's receiving her letter they were married under special licence at St Andrew's Church, Holborn.

It seems, then, that Corder inserted the advertisement for no other reason than that Mary Moore should answer it—but why he, or she, considered it necessary to effect a second introduction, and by the rather illicit means of a matrimonial advertisement, is a complete mystery.

The newly married couple settled down just outside London, at Grove House, Ealing Lane, Brentford, and Mary Corder started a girls' school. (The house was found for them by Thomas Griffiths Wainewright, who was an acquaintance of Corder's; an artist and probable murderer, Wainewright is the subject of Wilde's 'Pen, Pencil & Poison'. He thought of painting Mary Corder, but decided that her eyes 'baffled' him: 'they were like two lost stars that have strayed into a human face from the heavens'.)

For the short time they were together, Corder and his wife were very happy. According to Wainewright, 'Corder was inordinately fond of her and was for ever praising her virtues, squeezing her hand and whispering endearments to her. . . . I urged them to live on the continent.' Corder was to regret not taking this advice.

❍─❍─❍─❍─❍

During the early months of 1828 Anne Marten claimed that she was having a recurring dream in which she saw her stepdaughter being murdered and buried in the Red Barn. On

The murder in the Red Barn—a drawing by 'Phiz'

Saturday, 19 April, more to put an end to his wife's pestering than because he believed in clairvoyance, Thomas Marten searched the barn; noticing loose earth around some large stones, he started to dig and before long came upon a sack containing a badly decomposed body that was later identified as that of Maria Marten.

A warrant for Corder's arrest was issued, and he was soon traced to Brentford. Corder was taken back to Polstead for the inquest; on the way there, he and his escort stayed the night in a back room of the George Inn at Colchester. Before going to bed he was allowed to write a letter to his mother:

Dear Mother,
I scarcely dare to presume to address you, having a full knowledge of the shame, disgrace and, I may truly add, for ever, a stain upon my family, friends and late-formed connexions. I have but a few minutes to write; and being unfortunately labouring under this unfortunate charge, I have to solicit that you will receive Mr Moore [his wife's brother, a jeweller] on Friday morning, with whom, probably, may be my injured, lawful—and I must do her the justice to say— worthy and affectionate wife. I have always experienced from every branch of their family the kindest treatment—hope and trust that the same will be returned from you the short time they continue in this part of the country, which, I am sorry to have to state, is to hear the event of this dreadful catastrophe. I am happy to hear you are tolerable, considering the present circumstances. I may, perhaps, be allowed an interview with you in a day or two, but that, I find, is very uncertain. I must beg to subscribe myself your unfortunate, *though unworthy* son,
W. Corder

The words 'though unworthy' were crossed out, but were still legible. Corder afterwards said that he wished to burn the letter, but the police refused to allow this, and it was handed over to the prosecution as evidence.

After the inquest, at which the jury returned a verdict of wilful murder against him, Corder was taken to Bury St Edmunds Jail to await trial. On 28 April he wrote to Mary Corder:

My much injured and afflicted wife,
I arrived at this solitary prison on Friday, at ten o'clock at night, after a most dreadful day of misery. That night and the following day I was labouring under the most unimaginable affliction, alas! being confined by myself, without a single individual to ease me of my grief; on Saturday night I was quite worn out, and it pleased God to relieve me with sleep. The next morning (Sunday) I was summoned to attend

chapel; but I must first tell you, the minister brought me a
Bible and Prayer-Book on Saturday, and hearing of my awful
situation, a sermon was preached on the occasion; the text was
taken from 5th chap. 2nd Corinthians, 10th verse; the words
particularly reminded me of the Day of Judgement, where we
must all one day appear, and 'receive according to the deeds
done in the body whether good or bad'. . . . I cannot but
reflect upon the good advice which you have so often bestowed
upon me, a poor lost sinner, unworthy of any one blessing.
Yes, my dear wife, I feel persuaded my sins are more in
number than the hairs of my head. Were it possible, how
gladly would I fly to receive instructions from you, but alas!
the time is now past.

I have made application for you to visit me an hour or two
daily, thinking you might have taken lodgings at Bury; but
that favour, I find, is not allowed; so that I am altogether
deprived of my only earthly comfort, excepting through your
pen, from which I hope to derive some consolation; and by
searching the holy word of God, I hope to find forgiveness,
through the merits of Jesus Christ, who came into the world to
save sinners. Oh! that I may be one of the chosen people; yet
how can I expect his brightness to shine upon me, knowing
that I have always neglected to attend to his holy word. Our
minister has kindly offered me any of his religious books, for
on religion I must now build my hopes. My time is short—I
must soon depart from this vale of misery, and true it is, man
has but a short time to live, and even those who may now be in
a good flow of spirits and health, if they look over a short space
of time, they will be no more seen for ever. For my part, I
could wish it were tomorrow, but God's will must be done. I
cannot forget your severe affliction, and my dear mother's and
sister's. Were it not, my dear wife, for the afflictions of those I
have left behind, I should be better able to prepare myself for
another world. I have to entreat that you will write to my
sister, and as soon as you find yourself capable, visit them, for
I think perhaps you may, in some measure, be a comfort to
each other. . . .

With respect to this world, Mr and Miss Orridge [the prison
governor and his daughter] have offered me every favour their
regulations will admit of, and we are all allowed common
necessaries, with which I have reason to hope your good

brother will supply you, and I am anxious to hear how he was received at my mother's on Friday. When you feel disposed, come and see me, which I think had better not take place at present, as you will be allowed so few minutes with me, and that in the presence of a third person. Let me hear from you as soon as possible. I have not been able to write to mother, nor any of my friends. I shall be happy to receive a few lines from your brother, although I do not feel able to write to him. May God bless and protect you. I subscribe myself
Your unfortunate and almost broken-hearted husband,
William Corder

This letter, published after Corder's death, caused offence to many people. One commentator referred to its 'obscene juxtapositions', while another wrote:

What an incongruous animal is man!—how unsuitable are Corder's expressions in comparison with his character. The letter contains the effusions of a captured murderer, writhing under the pangs of guilt (for he says, 'I must soon depart from this vale of misery'). Upon what principle, therefore, can we reconcile his scriptural quotations, and his hope of becoming 'one of God's chosen people'? The tongue even of Charity is mute.

Corder's anxiety to ensure financial security for his wife, who was several months' pregnant, appeared in many of his letters. On 2 May he wrote:

My beloved wife,
As it is necessary to provide for the support of nature during the time we are in existence, I wish to know if you feel perfectly satisfied with respect to my property. . . . Remember, I have no one in this world but you to consult, and should it not be to your entire satisfaction, I entreat you to inform me. I am at liberty to make any alteration you think proper. I gave —— all the money I took with me, excepting three sovereigns, in consequence of the officers threatening to take it from me, saying I should pay my own expenses. I have several times attempted to write to my mother but this disgraceful

event prevents me. I cannot—I dare not address her.
Yours, &c.,

Wm. Corder

Mary Corder, who had by now taken lodgings in Bury St
Edmunds, was allowed to visit her husband. After she had visited
him on the morning of 3 May he wrote her a long letter expressing
his anticipation of an after-life; parenthetically, he begged her
'not even to look at a newspaper, as there are so many ready to
represent me in the blackest colours'. She replied the same day:

My dear husband,
I know that there are a number of idle reports published; but
when we consider that it is by such reports those who write
them get their living, it is a little excusable. Although no one
would like to have all their faults and every error painted in
their blackest colours to the world—pray be of good cheer, as
we are not to be judged by sinners like ourselves, but by one
who will pardon us if we repent. Look at the rich man and
Lazarus. Let me beg you to continue fervent in prayer, and end
them thus, 'Thy will, O Lord, and not mine be done.'
Write me a few lines every day, if ever so few—I am fearful
you do not eat—I have left all to follow you—let me know
what you want, and while I stay here, it shall only be to attend
to your comforts.
God bless you,
Adieu,

M. Corder

Mary Corder was a mixture of saintliness and practicality.
Shortly before returning to London to attend to some business
relating to Corder's property, she wrote to him:

Do not let the affairs of this world trouble you; I think the
sooner they are settled the better, as it will be a relief to you as
well as myself. I do not feel so happy when I stay away from
you, and I have endeavoured to conform to come once or twice
a week, as I fear it is troublesome to Mr Orridge. I am a little
more reconciled to my lot now, but cannot at present bear the
idea of seeing you so seldom. I will try at some future period.

We have never been separated since we were married, only once, for a day or two, and then, you know, a few hours appeared years; and now, what is it?—but the Lord fits the back to the burden; and we shall, I hope, be enabled to bear still greater troubles, if it be his will.

I shall be so happy when my mother has let the house, as she purposes coming to me—I wrote her last night. Let me entreat you not to think so much about me—I have One to protect me. When I was in London I could neither eat nor drink; it then cost very little to supply me with food. I now feel a great consolation at being so near you, and I wish our friends were also near us. I dare say some of them will come shortly. The time appears very long to us, but it will soon wear off. Adieu, God bless you.

Try and compose yourself—you would be surprised how I sleep; you have heard me say, if I have anything in the shape of trouble, I always sleep soundly—try and take pattern by me. You are very low-spirited today—but you know not what happiness awaits us both. Let me see tomorrow that you have profited by my advice—you will have a letter ready for me tomorrow.

Did you want the tea-spoon I sent you?—it is not borrowed—I bought or rather paid for it, and Mrs Kersey brought it; she generally sends every day to inquire after you—you see you are not forgotten by all. . . . Adieu, God bless you once more.
Your ever affectionate wife,

M. Corder

◶◶◶◶◶

The trial began on Thursday, 8 August. The surgeons who examined Maria Marten's body had adumbrated so many possible causes of death that the Crown elected to indict Corder on several counts, each a different method of murder, and including shooting, strangling, suffocating, stabbing, and even burying alive. The jury retired at ten minutes past two on the second day of the trial; they returned thirty-five minutes later with a verdict of guilty, and Lord Chief Baron Alexander set the execution for the following Monday.

On the eve of the execution, after seeing his wife for the last time, Corder was persuaded by Governor Orridge to make the following confession:

> Bury Gaol, Aug. 10, 1828,
> Condemned Cell.
> Sunday Evening, half-past 11.

I acknowledge being guilty of the death of poor Maria Marten, by shooting her with a pistol. The particulars are as follows:—
When we left her father's house we began quarrelling about the burial of the child, she apprehending that the place wherein it was deposited would be found out. The quarrel continued for about three-quarters of an hour, upon this and other subjects. A scuffle ensued, and during the scuffle, and at the time I think she had hold of me, I took the pistol from the side-pocket of my velveteen jacket, and fired. She fell, and died in an instant. I never saw even a struggle. I was overwhelmed with agitation and dismay. The body fell near the front doors on the floor of the barn. A vast quantity of blood issued from the wound, and ran on to the floor and through the crevices. Having determined to bury the body in the barn (about two hours after she was dead) I went and borrowed the spade of Mrs Stow; but before I went there, I dragged the body from the barn into the chaff-house, and locked up the barn. I returned again to the barn and began to dig the hole; but the spade being a bad one, and the earth firm and hard, I was obliged to go home for a pickaxe and a better spade, with which I dug the hole, and then buried the body. I think I dragged the body by the handkerchief that was tied round her neck. It was dark when I finished covering up the body.
I went the next day and washed the blood from off the barn floor. I declare to Almighty God I had no sharp instrument about me, and that no other wound but the one made by the pistol was inflicted by me.
I have been guilty of great idleness, and at times led a dissolute life, but I hope through the mercy of God to be forgiven.

> W. Corder
Witness to the signing by the said William Corder,
> John Orridge
> Sunday Evening, half-past
> 12 o'clock

While Corder was completing the confession, people were already arriving outside the prison to witness his hanging. According to the anonymous author of *An Authentic History of Maria Marten*:

By six [on Monday morning] vehicles of every description lined the streets, until every stable and yard was full, as were the inns and public-houses, so that adequate accommodation could not be afforded to man or beast, and hundreds who had not been provident enough to bring food with them were obliged to go to the place of execution hungry. The visitors consisted of every grade in society but there were more labouring men than any other class: for although it was a fine harvest-day, the reapers, &c., for miles around, 'struck', and came in gangs to witness the end of the murderer. Among the visitors were an extraordinary number from Polstead, who started from their places of abode at midnight.

Long before the hour arrived, every foot of ground was occupied in the pasture, and the buildings and trees which stood within view of the scene of death had their occupants.

At half past eleven o'clock, Mr Orridge announced to the prisoner that the time had arrived when he must resign himself to the officers of justice, and submit to the usual preparation for execution! Awful annunciation. Although Corder was well aware of the precise time fixed for his exit from this world (and he could see the minutes glide away by the prison dial which was within his view), he appeared to start when the announcement was made but he soon recovered himself, and earnestly called upon God for mercy.

He then took the arm of one of his attendants, and descended to a room immediately under his cell, where his arms were pinioned and his wrists tied by Foxton, the executioner who officiates at the metropolitan prison of Newgate. (Such was the certainty which the local authorities entertained of a conviction, that they sent 'a retaining fee' to the finisher of the law: and in order to ensure his important services, ordered him to proceed to Bury forthwith, and he actually started with a double set of furniture [ropes], as Jack [Ketch] calls them, before the prisoner was put upon his trial, and arrived at the place of destination twenty hours before it terminated.)

The procession was then formed in the usual manner, in order to advance towards the scaffold. Corder was sometimes at the side, and sometimes at the rear of the clergymen. His walk was not firm, neither could it be termed very unsteady, excepting when he once made a trip against a pebble. He was dressed exactly the same as on the days of the trial, with the exception of his having substituted a pair of speckled worsted stockings for the silk and cotton ones.

The executioner standing ready with the cap and rope in his hand, the prisoner was conducted to that fatal plank, from whence he was to be launched into an eternal world.

The prospect from the place where the wretched criminal stood is of the most beautiful description. The foreground consists of softly-swelling or gently-rising hills, which are bounded in the distance by extensive plantations of evergreens, so that they form a sort of picturesque amphitheatre round the prison. But to his view, upon whom the eyes of thousands were fixed, this lovely scene of romantic beauty had no charms; and almost as soon as he glanced upon it, it was shut from his sight for ever.

When the prisoner first made his appearance on the scaffold, there was a momentary buzz in the crowd, and all the men took off their hats.

The apparatus for the execution was exceedingly simple, and much smaller than the ponderous machine used at Newgate. Instead of being straight, the cross-beam is a kind of slender curve with holes perforated in it for the insertion of the rope.

When the prisoner beheld the executioner ready to receive him, the sight of the rope did not seem to be appalling, for he readily turned towards the minister of justice, and appeared anxious for the close of the dreadful scene.

After the cap had been drawn over his face, Mr Orridge spoke to him, and immediately told the executioner to turn it up. Mr Orridge then said to Corder that if he had any declaration to make, that was the time. At this moment, the prisoner seemed unable to stand, and an officer supported him. The greatest silence prevailed; but the crowd manifested an anxiety to know what the malefactor had said. Mr Orridge then advanced to the front of the platform, and in a loud voice proclaimed—'The prisoner acknowledges his sentence to be just, and declares that he dies in peace with all mankind!' A number of persons then said, 'Does he?—then may the Lord have mercy upon his soul!' After the executioner had fixed the rope to the beam, and was busy in tying what he calls the 'mysterious knot', it was suggested to him that he had left too much for what is technically called 'the fall', in consequence of which he reluctantly took part of it up, and it was quite evident that the executioner did not relish this interference with his public functions.

Everything being completely adjusted, the executioner descended from the scaffold, and just before the Reverend Chaplain had commenced his last prayer, he severed with a knife the rope which supported the platform, and Corder was cut off from the land of the living. Immediately he was suspended, the executioner grasped the culprit round the waist, in order to finish his earthly sufferings, which were at an end in a very few minutes. In his last agonies, the prisoner raised his hands several times; but the muscles soon relaxed, and they sank as low as the bandage round his arm would permit.

Immediately after the corpse had been taken into prison, there was a considerable scuffle among the spectators, numbers of whom wished to obtain a piece of the rope. That the cord made a considerable sum there can be no doubt, for when Foxton was questioned about his perquisites, he replied, 'What I got, I got, and that's all I shall say, except that that there was a very good rope.'

Foxton expressed his chagrin at having been interrupted in the performance of his professional duty. He said, 'I never like to be meddled with, because I always study the subjects which come under my hands, and, according as they are tall or short, heavy or light, I accommodate them with the fall. No man in England has had so much experience as me, or knows how to do his duty better.'

In the after part of the day, this public functionary visited the corpse in the Shire Hall, for the purpose of claiming Corder's trowsers, when he pointed to his handywork upon the neck of the criminal, and asked, exultingly, whether he had not 'done the job in a masterly manner'.

⊖⊖⊖⊖⊖

Corder's last letter was delivered to his wife shortly after the execution:

My life's loved Companion,
I am now going to the scaffold, and I have a lively hope of
obtaining mercy and pardon for my numerous offences. May
Heaven bless and protect you throughout this transitory vale of
misery, and when we meet again, may it be in the regions of
bliss! Adieu, my love, for ever adieu! In less than an hour I
hope to be in heaven. My last prayer is, that God will endue
you with patience, fortitude, and resignation to his Divine
will—rest assured that his wise providence will work all things
together for your good.
The awful sentence which has been passed upon me, and
which I am now summoned to answer, I confess is very just,
and I die in peace with all mankind. I feel truly grateful for
the kindnesses I have received from Mr Orridge, and for the
religious instruction and consolation I have received from the
Reverend Mr Stocking, who has promised to take my last
words to you.
Adieu.—W.C.

9 Spelling Mistakes

The ability to spell seems, at first sight, an unlikely prerequisite for committing the perfect murder, yet spelling mistakes have provided vital clues in a number of cases.

In 1917, Louis Voisin, a Belgian butcher working in London, was taken to Scotland Yard and asked by Chief Detective Inspector Frederick Wensley to write the words 'Bloody Belgium'; he wrote 'Bloody' as 'Blodie', the same mis-spelling as appeared on one of the parcels containing the dismembered remains of his mistress, Emilienne Gerard, and this led to his arrest and subsequent execution for her murder. Twenty-six years later, during another world war, a Luton lorry driver called Horace Manton murdered his wife and, after throwing her mutilated and unrecognisable body into a river, gave her a fake existence by writing letters over a semblance of her signature and posting them to her mother from London; but after three months a dyer's tag led to the body being identified, and Manton's spelling of 'Hampstead' without the medial *p*, as in the letters, was one of the several clues that added up to a verdict of guilty and the sentence of death. Most recently, Arthur Hosein, the elder of the two Indian brothers who abducted and murdered Mrs Muriel McKay, made the same spelling mistakes when writing words from police dictation as appeared in the ransom notes—'off' for 'of', 'discreetly' with only one *e*, 'occasion' with a double *s*, and 'existence' as 'existance'.

Perhaps the classic example of a criminal's guilt being proved by spelling mistakes is in the case of Irene May Wilkins, whose murder in 1921 smudged the respectability of Bournemouth, a town that had known only two murders in its history.

On 22 December, Miss Wilkins, a barrister's daughter who had served during the war in the Women's Army Auxiliary Corps and had afterwards worked as a cook, published an advertisement in the 'Situations Wanted' column of the *Morning Post*:

Lady Cook, 31, requires post in a school. Experienced in school with forty boarders. Disengaged. Salary £65. Miss Irene Wilkins, 21, Thirlmere Road, Streatham, S.W.16.

Before noon that day she received an answering telegram which read:

To Wilkins 21 Thirlmear Road London S.W.
Morning Post. Come immediately 4.30 train Waterloo.
Bournmouth Central. Car will meet train. Expence no object.
Urgent.
From Wood. Beech House.

Irene Wilkins at once wired back that she would travel down for an interview, and caught the 4.30 express from Waterloo. Soon after she had left home, her telegram was returned from Bournemouth where the post office had been unable to trace the name and address.

Just after daybreak on the following morning, a Friday, a labourer walking to work between Christchurch and Bournemouth noticed some cows nosing at something behind a clump of gorse bushes in a field. His curiosity aroused, he climbed over the fence and discovered the body of a woman lying face upwards; she had been killed by blows to the head from some heavy weapon. The labourer telephoned the police, who soon identified the dead woman as Irene Wilkins, reported missing by her widowed mother the night before. Her purse and attache case were missing. (They were found several days later in Branksome Park, about 8 miles away on the other side of Bournemouth. The purse was empty, but although the case had been ransacked, the contents, including a bundle of testimonial letters, were intact.) The clothing on the body was slightly damp, and as there had been no rain since about 8.30 the previous night, this gave the police a rough idea of the time of the crime. In the roadway were

A.

POST OFFICE TELEGRAPHS.
(Inland Telegrams.)

Prefix — Code —

Office of Origin and Service Instructions.

No. of Telegram

Words.	Sent
26	10.17
Charge.	At — To — By —

When a reply is to be prepaid, write the words "Reply Paid" in the space below. These words are not charged for.

TO Wilkins 21 Thirlmere Road
London S.W.

Morning post come immediately 4.30
train Waterloo Bournemouth Bristol Car
meet Grand Rush Expense no object
urgent

FROM Wood Beach House

This Name and Address of the Sender, IF NOT TO BE TELEGRAPHED, should be written in the space provided at the Back of the Form.

Allaway's telegram to Irene Wilkins

the tracks of a car running on Dunlop Magnum tyres, and by the extra depth of the treads it could be seen that the car had pulled up alongside the spot where the body was discovered.

Superintendent Shadrach Garrett took charge of the investigation, and immediately ordered a round-up of all cars in the district. Every owner-driver and chauffeur was questioned, with particular attention being given to drivers of cars with Dunlop Magnum tyres who had been out on the Thursday evening during the two hours following 7 o'clock, the time of arrival of the Waterloo express train at Bournemouth Central.

Garrett himself concentrated on the telegram that had lured Irene Wilkins to her death. In investigating this, two other such telegrams were found to have been sent, one on the 17th and the other on the 20th of that month; the girl who had received the first telegram had not answered the summons in person, but the second girl had travelled to Bournemouth only to return home when she found no one to meet her at the station.

All three telegrams were written by the same hand and contained spelling mistakes. In the first, that of 17 December, the word 'advertisement' had no second *e* and the word 'immediate' was spelt 'immidiate'; the medial *e* was missing from 'Bournemouth', 'if' had a double *f*, and 'expense' was spelt 'expence'.

In the telegram of 20 December the word 'pleasant' was spelt 'plesent', and due to the unusual structure of the letter *c*, 'car' looked like 'ear'.

In the third telegram, the one sent to Irene Wilkins on 22 December, mistakes and oddities in the first telegrams were repeated: there was no *e* in the word 'Bournemouth', *c* was written instead of *s* in 'expense', and 'car' again resembled 'ear'; although the writer had presumably copied the address from the *Morning Post*, 'Thirlmere' was spelt 'Thirlmear'.

✪✪✪✪✪

Some 22,000 documents relating to the case piled up at Bournemouth Police Station, but as the weeks dragged into months the chances of finding a solution seemed as slight as ever. By April Superintendent Garrett was convinced that he knew the guilty man but he had nothing like enough evidence to make an arrest. The man he suspected, Thomas Henry Allaway, was employed as a chauffeur by a wealthy family in one of the best parts of Bournemouth, and was known to the police as a deserter during the war and as a compulsive gambler afterwards.

Garrett decided to go through every file on the case, and his perseverance was rewarded by the discovery of a report that a subordinate had dismissed as irrelevant. This report, relating to information received from an engineer called Humphris, had come in early in January. It referred, among other things, to a Mercedes car, registration number LK 7405, that Humphris claimed to have seen outside Bournemouth Central Railway Station at about seven o'clock on the night of 22 December; according to the witness's recollection, a woman answering Irene Wilkins's description had entered the car and been driven away. Directly after the information from Humphris had been received, the Mercedes had been traced by the police, and its driver, Thomas Allaway, questioned. It had been noted that three of the car's tyres were Dunlop Magnums, the fourth a Michelin. The information from Humphris was so detailed that Allaway had been made to write out the three telegram messages from dictation, but as his handwriting was vertical, whereas the original telegrams were in a sloping hand, the report had been relegated to the limbo of a closed file.

Garrett set about obtaining specimens of Allaway's handwriting written before the murder. He made no secret of what he was after, and Allaway became more and more uneasy; as his uneasiness increased, so did the sums of money he gambled on horse races. On 20 April he stole his employer's cheque book and obtained about £20 by passing forged cheques to local tradesmen. Later that day, after despatching his wife and daughter to his wife's parents' home at Reading, he fled to London, assuming the name of T. Cook, which in the past he had used for postal betting transactions.

Garrett was delighted, of course, for it was now possible to apprehend Allaway for forgery and, holding him on that charge, to concentrate every effort on finding evidence to connect him with the murder of Irene Wilkins.

Allaway was arrested on 27 April. His wife, thinking that the charge was merely forgery, handed over to Garrett some old postcards, most of which had been written by Allaway from Germany, where he had served as a driver in the RASC during the war. There was also a long letter written to Mrs Allaway from Duren, in Germany, which was signed 'Your loving husband, Tom'. All these items were in the diagonal writing of the three telegrams and bore many of the characteristic mis-spellings. The most cogent document of all was the letter. When confronted with this, Allaway claimed that a fellow soldier had written it for him because of an injury to his wrist.

Allaway was picked out by several witnesses at an identity parade, and afterwards, instead of dictating an account of his movements on the evening of 22 December, he elected to write a statement. The remarkable thing about this statement was that the handwriting began in the acquired upright fashion and gradually relapsed into the sloping style of the telegrams. Later he was made to take down the three telegram messages from dictation, and although he was careful to maintain his upright hand, the spelling mistakes were there: 'plesent' for 'pleasant', 'Bournemouth' without the medial *e*, 'expense' with a *c*, and 'Thirlmear' for 'Thirlmere'.

☗☗☗☗☗

Allaway's luck had run out. He stood trial for the murder of Irene Wilkins at Winchester Assizes in July 1922 before Mr Justice Avory, who was not the most sentimental of judges. By the time it came for him to give evidence on his own behalf, he had resolved to deny that any of the correspondence to his wife was in his hand. But the futility of this blanket denial was quickly brought home to him when Horace Avory joined with Thomas Inskip, counsel for the prosecution, in cross-examining him:

Inskip: Take exhibit 23 [*a field postcard, dated 12 December 1918, addressed to Allaway's daughter Gladys, and reading: 'Dear baby, just a card hoping you are well as it leaves daddy at present lot of love Daddy xxxx'*]. Is that in your handwriting?

Allaway: (*A pause.*) I do not think that is mine. . . .

Avory: Will you swear it is not yours?

Allaway: It is addressed to my daughter, yes.

Avory: I did not ask you if it was to your daughter. Will you answer? Will you swear that it is not your handwriting?

Allaway: (*A pause.*) Yes, I will. I can't write like that. . . .

Inskip: Exhibit 19, is that yours?

Allaway: No, that is the same as the other.

Inskip: Now, if you turn to the back you will see a window marked with a cross. Do you recognise that house? Didn't you stop there?

Allaway: No, I do not recollect the name of the place.

Avory: 'Dear baby, I hope you are well, this is one of the places where daddy stopped, love from daddy, kiss momi for me.' You swear that is not your handwriting?

Allaway: It is not my handwriting at all. I can't write like that. . . .

Avory: Have you ever asked your wife for an explanation of her receiving postcards from somebody signed 'Tom', with kisses?

Allaway: No, I sent her a lot of postcards.

Avory: Have you any doubt that these are all in your hand-writing?

Allaway: Some of them are similar to my handwriting.

Inskip: Is that yours, exhibit 28?

Allaway: If this one is mine they are all mine. I cannot recognise the handwriting as mine. They are all to my wife, but I do not recollect writing them.

Inskip: Will you say, one way or the other, whether exhibit 28 is in your handwriting?

Allaway: I will say it is in my writing because it is very much like it.

Inskip: And you say if it is your handwriting the others must be?

Allaway: Yes.

Avory: Having just said that they are not?

Allaway: (*No reply.*)

Inskip: This exhibit 28 is dated 8 December 1918. 'This is the place where the Armistice terms were signed, also the German headquarters, there are still some left behind.' That is yours?

Allaway: That is not mine, that ain't. I have never been in the place where the Armistice was signed. . . .

Avory: Exhibit 43 is a letter written to your wife?

Allaway: Yes, it is.

Avory: Beginning 'Dearest May'?
Allaway: Yes.
Avory: And signed 'Your loving husband, Tom,' with kisses?
Allaway: Yes.
Avory: And kisses for the baby?
Allaway: Yes.
Avory: Now, won't you tell the truth about it? Is it not your letter?
Allaway: I have no recollection of sending it. I won't say I wrote it, because I don't recollect writing it.
Avory: 'Please send me some milk. I shall be going on a trip to Munster, which is about 150 miles from here. Today is Thursday. You should get this letter by Monday post. If you can possibly send it off by Tuesday I can call in at this place on the Sunday and take it back with me. We have got everything we want except milk and fags.' Isn't that the kind of thing you would write to your wife?
Allaway: (*A pause.*) Yes, I have wrote words to that effect.

⊖⊖⊖⊖⊖

The jury took only an hour to reach the verdict of guilty.

The Clerk of Assize intoned: 'Thomas Henry Allaway, you stand convicted of the crime of murder. Have you anything to say, or know you of anything why the Court here should not give you judgment of death according to law?'

But Allaway's ears were still ringing with the single word pronounced by the Foreman of the Jury. 'I beg pardon,' he murmured, 'I didn't quite catch the words.' The Clerk repeated them. 'I am innocent of this crime,' Allaway said. 'Absolutely.'

But nobody believed him: least of all, the judges of the Court of Criminal Appeal. He waited until the last moment, when there was no hope of a reprieve, before confessing his guilt.

Confession is said to be good for the soul, but it is unlikely to have had much effect in the case of Allaway, who seems to have displayed the same indifference to his own death as to that of Irene Wilkins. During the three months he spent in prison he slept like a top and ate like a horse, so that by the time of his execution, on 19 August, he had put on ten pounds in weight.

One should, I suppose, in order to be fashionably liberal, express sorrow at the fact that the execution, carried out by the normally reliable Ellis, did not go altogether smoothly. The noose shifted and Allaway died from strangulation, thrashing around in the pit, instead of from the prescribed broken neck. At the inquest, the prison doctor, when asked the formal question of whether death was instantaneous, replied with a piece of true British understatement:

'Almost so,' he said.

10 Starr Faithfull

Early in the morning of Monday, 8 June 1931, a beachcomber
called Daniel Moriarty came upon the body of twenty-five-year-
old Starr Faithfull amidst the refuse and seaweed on the sands of
Long Beach, Long Island, near New York; she was wearing only
a black-and-white foulard dress and silk stockings. No doubt if
she had had some less romantic-sounding name, her death would
have rated no more than a few inches of space on the inside pages
of the New York newspapers, and the inquest would have been
a brief formality preceding a verdict of accidental death by
drowning. But the discovery of the body was made front page
news, with the name giving a sort of poetry to the banner head-
lines. Elvin N. Edwards, the District Attorney of Nassau County,
in which Long Beach is situated, saw the case as a heaven-sent
opportunity to continue the self-advertising campaign which he
had inaugurated during the recent prosecution of a gangster
called 'Two-Gun' Crowley. 'This is a case of murder,' he de-
clared at his first press conference, and at subsequent daily con-
ferences (at which he almost invariably arrived 'laden with fresh
clews') kept the publicity pot boiling with statements like, 'I
expect an arrest to be made within twenty-four hours' and 'I
know the identity of the two men who killed Starr Faithfull—one
of them is a prominent New York politician'.

On 11 June, after two post-mortem examinations had been
conducted, Edwards decided to have a third—for no other reason,
it seems, than to stage a dramatic interruption of the funeral. This
third examination did not help at all to clarify the earlier findings,
which appeared to support not just one theory but all three:
accident, suicide, *and* murder. The body was thought to have
been in the water for about forty-eight hours (this was the esti-

mate of the most experienced of the pathologists; other medico-legal experts inferred a shorter period). The presence of water in the lungs showed that the girl had drowned. She had eaten a large meal about four hours before death. There were numerous bruises; most of them, it was believed, had been caused by driftwood, but others had probably been inflicted while she was alive.

Starr Faithfull—a sketch by Rudolph Haybrook

Toxicological analysis revealed that she had taken a heavy dose of veronal, a barbiturate, which would have induced stupor or semi-stupor; it was unlikely, therefore, that the drowning was a deliberate act. At first it was thought that she had been raped, but the second examination modified this finding to that of sexual intercourse.

While Edwards strained his larynx and his imagination, the Faithfull family—mother, English-born step-father Stanley Faithfull, and younger daughter Tucker—were besieged by reporters and sob sisters in their apartment at 12 St Luke's Place, Greenwich Village, three doors from the home of Mayor James J. Walker. Stanley Faithfull did most of the talking; according to him, Starr was the soul of conventionality, a home-loving girl whose idea of fun was to sit by the fireside and read books on philosophy. But before long it became clear that the step-father was a reckless liar; virtually every statement he made was the opposite of the truth. As the press and the police delved into Starr Faithfull's past, a sensational picture emerged.

At the age of eleven she was seduced by Andrew J. Peters, a former mayor of Boston, congressman, and Assistant Secretary of the Treasury; this elderly friend of the family used ether to arouse her senses, and she became addicted to the drug. Peters (who at the time of Starr's death was strongly tipped as the next governor of Massachusetts) denied the allegations, but there was a surfeit of evidence: Starr's 'mem book', composed largely of unpublishable pornography, contained details of their trips together ('Spent night AJP Providence. Oh, Horror, Horror, Horror!!!'); there were photostats of hotel registers; there was a payment of $20,000 to the Faithfull family for a formal release, absolving Peters of all liability for damage done to Starr. This was a small price to pay. From the mem book, and from the recollections of people who had known her, Starr's tragically confused personality was revealed. She was a nymphomaniac who abhorred the sexual act; although prudish about dress (she wore ankle-length dresses during the flapper era, thought bathing suits immoral, and had a horror of being seen in bare feet), a few drinks intoxicated her and she had been known to undress and perform erotic dances at parties. She had been treated by several psychiatrists, and at the age of nineteen had spent nine days in a sanatorium. A year before her death, a policeman, summoned by people who had heard screams, found her naked and beaten-up in a hotel room; the man with her, who called himself Joseph Collins, was told to leave, and she was taken to Bellevue Hospital. The hospital record read:

> Brought to hospital by Flower Hospital ambulance. Noisy and unsteady. Acute alcoholism. Contusions face, jaw, and upper lip. Given medication. Went to sleep. Next a.m. noisy, crying. People came. Discharged.

Her own statement read:

> I was drinking gin as far as I know. This is the first time I have had anything to drink for six months. I don't know how many I had. I don't remember. I suppose somebody knocked me around a bit.

An inveterate—indeed, obsessional—traveller, she visited England three times, first in the summer of 1928, again the following summer, and then, with her mother and sister, in the summer and autumn of 1930; on the last two occasions she stayed most of the time at cheap hotels and boarding houses in the Chelsea and Kensington districts of London. During the 1929 visit, according to a friend, she was 'frequently intoxicated and once rode to her hotel in the early morning clad only in her pyjamas'; also during this visit, after an argument with an admirer called Dennis Barnett, she attempted suicide in her room at the Greyfriars Hotel by taking an overdose of allonal. Shortly after this incident, she and Rudolph Haybrook, an artist friend, created a disturbance in her room, and she was asked to leave the hotel. In a letter to her mother, she explained:

> R.H., the artist, was a bit too rough. When a person is beastly, I get that way myself, and the result was too damn noisy so that the landlord complained.
> I am all settled in the new house, namely, the Commodore

Hotel, 4 Pembroke Square. I told you about D.B. He is buying
a car and is really trying so hard to make up for being 'nasty to
Susie' that she has forgiven him practically. Cheerioski.

And in another letter:

If Mr Stackpoole [manager of the Greyfriars Hotel] was better
looking I would heap coals of fire on his head by asking him to
dinner at the Commodore. He looks exactly like a match
before it's lit. . . .
About my amours, I have none at present, as I am going
through a very platonic phase starting after my row with D.B.
The last I saw him I told him he looked like a plump bird with
big wondering eyes. I am having him to dinner tonight and
afterwards drive in his new car.
My other lovers [this word is circled] are away. I had a blind
date the other night with a friend of Derek Dawson, but he
was too fragile to appeal to me.
Did I ever tell you that a man named Lord Brendon wanted
me to go to Buda Pest (how in hell do you spell it?). Also D.B.
begged me to live with him in his new flat.
As I told you, I have become very platonic. It is a great state
to be in.

From the end of November 1930, when she returned to New
York after the third visit to England, she corresponded regularly
with friends in London.

We are somewhere between Seventh- and Eighth-Avenues—
not a very polite part of town. Our front room looks out on a
city playground filled with God's horrid little creatures. If ever
you see a play called 'Street Scene', you will know our
environment. . . .
I wish I could feel more kindly about ——. He seems to me a
sort of living symbol of futility—or the unimportance of being
earnest. If it is true that nothing succeeds like success, it is
also true that nothing fails so completely as a failure. I am
certainly far from being one to talk—but I can't help it. . . .

Life is most depressing. I wish I were starving without a

shilling for gas in Bramerton Street [Chelsea], with the roof
falling in and rain pouring in—anything but this.
Do you know where I wish I was at this moment? I wish I
were having a nice, long double-whisky with you at the Six
Bells [Chelsea].
Everything now seems so arid, barren, blank, negative, and
futile. I wish I were at the World's End [another public house
in Chelsea], and that some geographical phenomenon would
wipe America off the map.
Please button up your overcoat, be careful crossing streets, and
in every way take good care of yourself. At present I can't
believe that anyone like your charming, brilliant self ever
existed. You are so far removed from this maelstrom and all
its low-down inhabitants.

In practically every letter you say, '*Be good.*' You should just
see how damnably *good* I've become. . . . *Never, never* again
shall I be the worse for drink, or anything else one swallows or
inhales.
I want to go on a terrific, wild, and champagney 'bender'.
Being good is all very well when one is fat—but now I'm thin,
we shall see. . . .
This spring, in London, we will all look in the opposite
direction from Heaven for a change, and discard wings, halos,
etc.
Not that it's frightfully interesting, *but*—I have lost
twenty-five pounds! Gone is the bloated ox, swollen whale,
elephant, or what-have-you which used to trot so eagerly to
Wood's after Bourbon biscuits or to the Cadogan Arms for
beer. We did consume some beer last summer. I dread to think
what would happen if I should live in Berlin.

I am more and more bored by my native land. If I were a man
I would join the Foreign Legion and forget my past.
I am living on tea and tomatoes, and day by day the scale
creaks less as my (not so elephantine) physique bears down on
it. When you see the new figure it will positively explode with
grace. It won't be long either! Yeah, sez me!!
Yesterday I swear I was completely overcome by depression.
New York seemed like a huge graveyard, and the skyline
didn't thrill me a bit. It just looked like a lot of elongated

dominoes and perfectly ridiculous.

Everything here seems like a most awful anti-climax. I realize that my depressed attitude is far from admirable, but if I 'made an effort' I think it would be like bursting a blood vessel mentally.

I am so anxious to cheer you up—and yet I can't think of much except that we are all only living in the FUTURE—that is, when we sail for dear old London, and see darling old you. . . .

Don't worry about ——. When we are nineteen we say all sorts of things. I have an old diary which proves that!

I value your peace of mind, happiness, whatever you choose to call it, as much as I do my own. It is one of the few *un*selfish feelings I've ever had for anyone.

She wrote to Rudolph Haybrook in the first week of May 1931:

How does the old busy bee improve his hour these days, and is he having fun? Let me know.

I have my passage booked in the Franconia, sailing from New York, May 30. A friend of mine is sailing in that boat, which explains my decision. Tucker will undoubtedly sail before this. After the boat has passed the Statue of Liberty I shall believe in God, fairies, Santa Claus, and so on. Oh yeah? Yeah!

ooooo

Some time in 1928 Starr Faithfull had met and fallen in love with George Jameson Carr, a Scottish surgeon on the Cunard liner, the SS *Franconia*. While not oblivious to her charms, Carr was certainly at times embarrassed by her attentions: never more so than on 29 May 1931, when she boarded the *Franconia* in Manhattan docks shortly before sailing time. In her letter to Rudolph Haybrook, quoted above, she had spoken of returning to England on this vessel, but the family funds were far too low to finance the trip. She was drunk when she came aboard, ostensibly to say goodbye to Carr. After a scene in his cabin during which she became hysterical, he insisted that she leave.

Instead of going ashore, however, she mingled with the passengers and the *Franconia* was under way before her presence was discovered. The liner was stopped and, struggling and screaming, she was lifted down into a tug which took her back to New York.

A week after this incident, on 5 June, she was again removed from an England-bound liner, the *Mauretania*, but this time she was taken off well before sailing time. She was last seen by any known witness in the evening of that day, still in the area of the docks. A few hours later she was drowned.

⊖⊖⊖⊖⊖

The riddle of her death seemed to be solved when, towards the end of June, George Jameson Carr returned to New York. He brought with him three letters written by Starr. The first letter, on Hotel Plaza notepaper, was postmarked from New York at 6pm on 30 May, the day after the *Franconia* incident; there was no salutation.

I am going (definitely now—I've been thinking of it for a long time) to end my worthless, disorderly bore of an existence— before I ruin anyone else's life as well. I certainly have made a sordid, futureless mess of it all. I am dead, dead sick of it. It is no one's fault but my own—I hate everything so—life is HORRIBLE [this word is underlined twice].
Being a sane person you may not understand—I take dope to forget and drink to try and like people but it is no use. I am mad and insane over you. I hold my breath to try to stand it—take allonal in the hope of waking happier but that *homesick* feeling never leaves me.—I have, strangely enough, more of a feeling of peace or whatever you call it now that I know it will soon be over. The half hour before I die will, I imagine, be quite blissful.
You promised to come and see me. I realize ABSOLUTELY that it will be the one and only time. There is no earthly reason why you should come. If you do it will be what I call an act of marvellous generosity and kindness.
What I did yesterday was very horrible. Although I don't see how you could lose your job as it must have been clearly seen

what a nuisance you thought me.
If I don't see you again—goodbye. Sorry to so lose all sense of
humour. But I am suffering so that all I want is to have it over
with. It's become a hell such as I couldn't have imagined.
If you come to see me when you are in this time you will be a
sport—you are assured by this letter of no more bother from
me.
My dear,

Starr

The second letter was a formal apology, intended for Carr to
show to his superiors. Written on the stationery of the Hotel
Pennsylvania, it was postmarked from New York at 8pm on
2 June.

Dear Dr. Carr:
I want to apologise and to tell you how deeply I regret my
conduct on the *Franconia* last Friday.—I had come down
hoping to renew our acquaintance but I fear I only made a
fool of myself and that it was very disagreeable for you.—I had
brought some drinks onto the boat with me, and drank them
too fast. I become utterly irrational when I drink, and I want
you to know how deeply sorry I am for the embarrassment I
must have caused you.
Very sincerely,

Starr Faithfull

The third and last letter, written on the stationery of Lord &
Taylor, the Fifth Avenue department store, was postmarked at
4pm on 4 June, the day before she disappeared.

Hello Bill Old Thing:
It's all up with me now. This is something I am GOING to
put through. The only thing that bothers me about it, the only
thing I dread, is being outwitted and prevented from doing
this—which is the only possible thing for me to do. If one
wants to get away with murder one has to jolly well keep one's
wits about one. It's the same with suicide. If I don't watch out
I will wake up in a psychopathic ward, but I intend to watch
out and accomplish my end this time.

No ether, allonal or window jumping. I don't want to be maimed. I want oblivion. If there is an after life it would be a dirty trick—but I'm sure fifty million priests ARE wrong. That is one of the things one *knows*. Nothing makes any difference now. I love to eat and can have one delicious meal with no worry over gaining. I adore music and I am going to hear some good music. I believe I love music more than anything. I am going to drink *slowly* keeping *AWARE* every second. Also I am going to enjoy my last cigarettes,—I won't worry because men flirt with me in the streets—I shall encourage them—I don't care who they are. I wish I got more pleasure with men.

It's a great life when one has 24 hours to live. I can be rude to people—I can tell them they are too fat or that I don't like their clothes, and I don't have to dread being a lonely old woman, or poverty, obscurity, or boredom. I don't have to dread living on without ever seeing you, or hearing rumours such as 'The women all fall for him'—and 'he entertains charmingly'. Why in hell shouldn't you!—But it's more than I can cope with—this feeling I have for you. I have tried to pose as clever and intellectual thereby to attract you, but it was not successful and I couldn't go on writing those long, studied letters. I don't have to worry because there are no words in which to describe this feeling I have for you. The words Love, adore, worship have become meaningless.—There is nothing I can do but what I am going to do. I shall never see you again. That is extraordinary. Although I can't comprehend it any more than I can comprehend the words—'always' or 'time'. They produce a very merciful numbness.

Starr

At the time, the last letter was taken as proof that Starr Faithfull had committed suicide, and it was assumed that she had hidden aboard a liner and thrown herself into the sea near Long Beach. But this theory leaves several questions unanswered: most important, perhaps, what happened to her missing clothes and handbag, which were never found; and how, when heavily drugged, was she able to commit such a deliberate, premeditated act of self-destruction?

Can it be that, with an irony she herself would have savoured, Starr Faithfull was murdered before she could accomplish her

No pistol, alcohol, or window jumping.
I don't want to be maimed. I want
oblivion. If there is an after life
it would be a dirty Trick - but
I'm sure fifty million priests are
wrong. That is one of those Things
one knows. Nothing makes any
difference now. I love to eat and
can have one delicious meal with no
worry over gaining I adore music
and I am going to hear some good
music. I believe I love music more
than anything. I am going to
drink slowly keeping AWARE
every second. Also I am going
to say my last cigarettes, -
I won't worry because nuns
exist with us in the streets - I
shall succour them - I don't
care who They are. I wish

Starr Faithfull's last letter, second page

shouldn't you!. But its more than I can cope with this feeling I have for you. I have tried to pose as clever and intellectual thereby to attract you, but it was not successful and I couldn't go on writing those long, studied letters. I don't have to worry, because there are no words in which to describe this feeling I have for you. The words Love, adore, worship have become meaningless. — There is nothing I can do but what I am going to do.

I shall never see you again. That is extraordinary. Although I can comprehend it any more than I can comprehend the words "always". or "time". They produce a very merciful numbness.

Starr.

Starr Faithfull's last letter, fourth page

intention to commit suicide? Bearing in mind the hotel-room incidents involving Joseph Collins and Rudolph Haybrook, it seems at least possible that the vital clue to the mystery is contained in her last letter:

> I won't worry because men flirt with me on the streets—I shall encourage them—I don't care who they are. I wish I got more pleasure with men. . . .

11 Newgate Finale

Charlotte Cheeseman, known to her friends as 'Lottie', was a stripper: but not in the sense that she divested herself in public. In the cigar-making industry a stripper is a person trained to remove the centre stalk from tobacco leaves, and in 1902, the year of her death, Lottie was employed as such by a firm at Hoxton in the east end of London.

For some time she had 'walked out' with a soldier called Joseph Bruce, but he saw little of her after she became acquainted with George Woolfe, a denizen of the Shoreditch ghetto whose personal charm was no more pleasing than his appearance—which, by all accounts, was repulsive. Unaccountably, she soon became infatuated with Woolfe and, trusting his promise of marriage, went to bed with him.

Perhaps she was made pregnant; perhaps, in her naivety, she believed that pregnancy was an invariable consequence of deflowered virginity; or perhaps, unexpectant but impatient to be married, she lied to Woolfe about her condition in the cause of hastening their union. At all events, her hopes that he would do the decent and promised thing suffered a brutal blow when he wrote to her in the first week of 1902:

Miss Cheeseman,
Just a line. On Monday morning I made the acquaintance of a young lady who I admire much better than you; therefore you had better do the same and think no more of me. I hope you will take this as goodbye for good.

G. Woolfe

P.S. I hope I shall never hear of you or see you again, as I am indeed thankful I have got rid of you so easily. I have got the date I went to you, so if you find yourself in any trouble, or I mean in a certain condition, it will be no good to put the blame on me, so forget me and never think any more of me. I pity the man who ever gets tied up to you, but I am glad that I am free at last and I have now the chance of being my old self again.

Lottie's love outweighed her pride, and she wrote back at once, pleading with him to 'make it up' and even going to the trouble of composing a verse:

> My pen is blunt, my ink is pale,
> My love for you will never fail,
> Apples is ripe,
> Pears is better,
> George, dear, will you answer this letter?

Woolfe reacted savagely to Lottie's appeal by writing to her employer, giving as an address 218 Southgate Road, Kingsland, and signing the letter 'Alfred Dixon':

Dear Sir,
Excuse me, you have a young woman in your employ named Charlotte Cheeseman and I think it only right that you should be aware of her character. I send this letter to you to inform you that she is in the habit of taking home cigars and quantities of tobacco leaf and to let you know she was discharged from Lipton's for stealing tea. She was also discharged from Salmon & Gluckstein for stealing five cigars, and before entering your employment she worked for an old lady in the Southgate Road, but was only there five days on account of her thieving habits and drunkenness. About six weeks ago she lost two days at your firm on account of having a black eye and these are her habits at every firm she works. I am not sure of the quantity of cigars she had taken from your firm, but tobacco leaf I have seen her with a pocketful. I will be only too pleased to give you further information in regard to her character and so will the old lady she so cruelly wronged.

The cigar maker called in the police, who discovered that the address was non-existent and that the girl's previous employers had all found her honest.

Even if Lottie Cheeseman did not recognise the handwriting of the letter, which seems unlikely, she could hardly have failed to guess the identity of the sender; but still she believed that she could recapture Woolfe's affection—and, surprisingly, she wanted to. Receiving no response to her written appeals, she called on him one evening, but Woolfe abused her and struck her across the face. News of this incident reached her ex-beau Joseph Bruce, who was still on friendly terms with her, and he sought out Woolfe with the intention of paying him back; Woolfe, however, calmly produced one of the pathetic letters from Lottie:

Dear George,
Don't be offended because I am writing this letter to you. Will you go out with me again, as you know what you have done to me. I think it is a shame how you have treated me, but I will forget that and think of you all the more. You don't know how much I love you.

Bruce read this letter, but whether he understood it is another matter, for he told Woolfe that he would have nothing more to do with the girl, and they parted amicably.

Lottie continued to write to Woolfe, at least one letter a day, and eventually he agreed to meet her again. On Saturday night, 25 January 1902, they were seen together in the bar of the Rosemary Branch in Southgate Road; Lottie had gone to some trouble to look at her best and was wearing a new green coat.

The following morning, a group of boys were playing football on the waterlogged wastes of Tottenham Marshes, a place of ill repute that had once been the haunt of highwaymen and cut-purses and was now the resort of gangs of east end hooligans. One of the boys kicked the ball too enthusiastically and it landed in a ditch beside the dead body of Lottie Cheeseman. Her face was a mask of frozen blood; her skull had been battered in and her nose broken, seemingly with a heavy chisel, yet according to the doctor who carried out the post-mortem examination, death had only been gradual.

The day after the discovery of the murder, Woolfe enlisted in the Surrey Regiment in the name of Slater. When he was arrested on 6 February he still had scratches on his face, mute evidence of the girl's efforts to resist his attack. At the trial Sir Richard Muir, who led for the prosecution, used the letters with deadly effect to establish the motive for the crime, and Woolfe was found guilty and sentenced to death.

As Muir left the court he remarked to his clerk:

'I am very glad I have had the opportunity of putting that young gentleman into the condemned cell. He will know what it is to suffer before the hangman comes for him.'

Woolfe was the last murderer to be executed at Newgate before the ancient prison was demolished. Few of the earlier miscreants descended through the gallows floor to a more deserving death than his.

12 Edith Thompson

On the evening of Tuesday, 3 October 1922, Percy Thompson, a thirty-two-year-old shipping clerk, took his wife Edith to the Criterion Theatre to see Cyril Maude in *The Dippers*. At about midnight, as they were walking from Ilford Station to their home at 41 Kensington Gardens, a young man appeared from the shadows and, after a few words of altercation, stabbed Thompson several times in the body and twice in the neck.

'Oh, don't. Oh, don't,' Edith Thompson was heard to cry out.

The young man fled. Leaving her husband sprawled on the pavement, Mrs Thompson ran back towards the railway station, and to the first people she met she screamed: 'Oh, my God! Will you help me? My husband is ill. He is bleeding.'

By the time a doctor arrived, Percy Thompson was dead.

○-○-○-○-○

The murderer was Frederick Edward Francis Bywaters, a ship's writer on leave from the P & O liner, the SS *Morea*, which had docked at Gravesend on 23 September. He was twenty, eight years younger than Edith Thompson, who had been his lover for some eighteen months.

On 5 October, after several hours of questioning, Mrs Thompson made a long statement to the police, who by this time, acting on information received from her relatives, had apprehended and detained Bywaters. When she made the statement, she had no idea that Bywaters was in custody. Her sole concern was to shield him, and in describing the murder, she gave the impression that Percy Thompson had been attacked by an invisible man:

When we got between De Vere and Endsleigh Gardens (we were walking on the right-hand side) my husband suddenly went into the roadway, I went after him, and he fell up against me, and called out 'oo-er'. He was staggering, he was bleeding, and I thought that the blood was coming from his mouth. I cannot remember whether I saw anyone else there or not. I know there was none there when he staggered up against me. I got hold of my husband with both hands and assisted him to get up against the wall. He stood there for about a minute or two and then slid down on to the footway, he never spoke.

Later in the same statement she referred to Bywaters for the first time, and it is fascinating to observe how, accompanying her gradual realisation of the futility of denying what the police already knew or would easily find out, her words progressed towards an almost complete confession of her relationship with the young man:

I know Freddie Bywaters, I have known him for several years; we were at school together, at least I wasn't but my two brothers were. . . . He has been for a very long time on visiting terms with my family. In June, 1921, Bywaters came to reside with my husband and myself. . . . He came as a paying guest. I think he paid 25s. or 27s. 6d. per week. He was with us up to the beginning of August, 1921. I remember August Bank Holiday, 1921. My husband and I quarrelled about something, he struck me. I knocked a chair over. Freddie came in and interfered on my behalf. I left the room and I do not know what transpired between them. As far as my recollection goes, Freddie left on the following Friday, but before he left my husband and he were friends again. We have been in the habit of corresponding with one another. His letters to me and mine to him were couched in affectionate terms. I am not in possession of any letters he writes to me. I have destroyed all as is customary with me with all my correspondence. . . . When he was at home in England, we were in the habit of going out occasionally together without my husband's knowledge.

After making this statement she was taken from the CID office to the matron's room and—possibly by accident, almost certainly by police design—she caught a glimpse of Bywaters waiting in the library. The shock broke her resistance. 'Oh God, oh God, what can I do?' she moaned. 'Why did he do it? I did not want him to do it. I must tell the truth.' She was hurried back to the CID office, where she made a brief statement naming Bywaters as her husband's assailant.

Soon afterwards, Bywaters was told that both he and Mrs Thompson would be charged with murder. 'Why her?' he asked. 'She was not aware of my movements.' After being cautioned, he stated:

I left Manor Park at 11 p.m. and proceeded to Ilford. [He had visited the home of Edith's mother at Manor Park, spending most of the evening with Avis Graydon, Edith's unmarried sister, who had been his 'young lady' until the affair with Edith began.] I waited for Mrs Thompson and her husband. When near Endsleigh Gardens I pushed her to one side, also pushing him further up the street. I said to him, 'You have got to separate from your wife.' He said, 'No.' I said, 'You will have to.' We struggled. I took my knife from my pocket and we fought and he got the worst of it. Mrs Thompson must have been spellbound for I saw nothing of her during the fight. . . . The reason I fought with Thompson was because he never acted like a man to his wife. He always seemed several degrees lower than a snake. I loved her and I could not go on seeing her leading that life. I did not intend to kill him. I only meant to injure him. I gave him an opportunity of standing up to me as a man but he wouldn't. I have had the knife some time; it was a sheath knife. I threw it down a drain when I was running through Endsleigh Gardens.

When the charges were laid, the police had already come across one or two letters from Edith Thompson to Bywaters, which showed the intimacy of their relationship; but on 12 October the young man's ditty box was unlocked and found to contain many more letters that he had received from her while he was serving aboard the SS *Morea* on four voyages, each of about two months' duration, since November 1921. These letters (which were signed 'Peidi', a pet-name probably derived from 'Edie', and nearly all written from the office of the Aldersgate millinery firm where she worked as a book-keeper) contained passages that seemed not only to strengthen immeasurably the police case against Mrs Thompson on the three indictments of conspiring, soliciting and inciting to murder, but also to justify two further indictments: administering poison with intent to murder her husband and administering a destructive thing—namely, broken glass—with the same intent.

⊖⊖⊖⊖⊖

To those who believe that Edith Thompson was innocent, the letters are no more than symptoms of her romanticism; they prove only that she lived in a world of make-believe. More specifically, her champions assert that the references in the letters to the administration of poison and powdered glass to her husband were demonstrated to be Mitty-esque inventions by Sir Bernard Spilsbury's negative findings at the post-mortem: but this point loses validity when one reads Spilsbury's testimony. What he said was this:

> If glass had been administered I would not necessarily expect to find indications in the organs. . . . It would pass away in the food and in the excrement. . . . As to other poisons, I would not expect necessarily to find indications of poisons if they had been administered some considerable time before. Some poisons would leave no traces at any time even if death occurred shortly after administration. Others would produce effects which would last for a few days, and in the case of a few poisons a few weeks, but after the end of that time there are very few poisons which would leave any indications, except poisons which were corrosive or which were markedly irritant poisons.

In the following extracts, which make up a minute, and perhaps unrepresentative, sample of the whole correspondence, italics indicate that a passage was quoted by Sir Thomas Inskip, the Solicitor General, in his opening speech for the prosecution at the trial; leaving aside the question of whether or not Edith Thompson administered poison or powdered glass to her husband, these passages were important, Inskip said, 'to show that she so worked and preyed on the mind of this young man by her suggestions that, although it was his hand that struck the blow, it was her mind that conceived the crime'.

Mid-November 1921:
Darlint,—Its Friday today—that loose end sort of day (without you) preceding the inevitable week end. I dont know what to do—to just stop thinking, thinking very very sad thoughts darlint, they will come, I try to stifle them, but its no use. . . . All I could think about last night was that compact we made. Shall we have to carry it thro'? dont let us darlint. Id like to live and be happy—not for a little while, but for all the while you still love me. Death seemed horrible last night—when you think about it darlint, it does seem a horrible thing to die, when you have never been happy really happy for one little minute. . . .
Yesterday I met a woman who had lost 3 husbands in eleven years and not thro the war, 2 were drowned and one committed suicide and some people I know cant lose one. How unfair everything is. Bess and Reg are coming to dinner Sunday. . . .

End of November 1921:
'It is the man who has no right, who generally comforts the woman who has wrongs.' This is also right darlint isnt it? as things are, but darlint, its not always going to be is it? You will have the right soon wont you? Say Yes. . . .
Last Tuesday when Avis came across he asked her to teach him [to dance] and she is coming across next Tuesday to give him his first lesson. He wanted me to teach him, but I said I hadnt the patience, my days of dragging round beginners were over. Of course this conversation led to us discussing dancing rather a lot and we talked about the nonstop. We were talking of going as a set with our own partners and Avis detailed them all until she came to me and hesitated so I filled in the gap by saying 'Bill', I felt like telling him who it really was and perhaps had Avis not been there I should have done, but I didnt want to endure any more scenes especially in front of her. . . .
I gave way this week (to him I mean), its the first time since you have been gone. Why do I tell you this? I dont really know myself. . . .

10 February 1922:
Darlint—You must do something this time—I'm not really
impatient—but opportunities come and go by—they have to—
because I'm helpless and I think and think and think—perhaps—it
will never come again.
I want to tell you about this. On Wednesday we had words—in
bed—Oh you know darlint—over that same old subject and he
said—it was all through you I'd altered.
I told him if he ever again blamed you to me for any difference
there might be in me, I'd leave the house that minute and this is
not an idle threat.
He said lots of other things and I bit my lip—so that I shouldn't
answer—eventually went to sleep. About 2 a.m. he woke me up
and asked for water as he felt ill. I got it for him and asked him
what the matter was and this is what he told me—whether its the
truth I dont know or whether he did it to frighten me, anyway it
didnt. He said—someone he knows in town . . . had given him a
prescription for a draught for insomnia and he'd had it made up
and taken it and it made him ill. He certainly looked ill and his
eyes were glassy. I've hunted for the said prescription everywhere
and cant find it and asked him what he had done with it and he
said the chemist kept it.
I told Avis about the incident only I told her as if it frightened
and worried me as I thought perhaps it might be useful at some
future time that I had told somebody.
What do you think, darlint. His sister Maggie came in last night
and he told her, so now there are two witnesses, altho' I wish he
hadn't told her—but left me to do it.
It would be so easy darlint—if I had things—I do hope I shall.
How about cigarettes?
Have enclosed cuttings of Dr. Wallis's case. It might prove
interesting darlint, I want to have you only I love you so much
try and help me—Peidi.

The cuttings referred to a case at Litchfield in which the clerical
member of a *ménage à trois* formed by a curate, his wife, and a
ship's surgeon called Wallis, had died mysteriously from hyoscine
poisoning. Many other press cuttings were enclosed with Edith
Thompson's letters to Bywaters; some ('Chicken Broth Death',
'University Mystery of Poisoned Sweets' and 'Girl's Death

Riddle') seemed to support the prosecution case, while others
('Do Men like Red Haired Women?', 'Fuel Control and Love
Making' and 'The Ideal Dance Partner') had no apparent lethal
undertones.

22 February 1922:
Darlingest boy, it is four whole weeks today since you went
and there is still another four more to go—I wish I could go to
sleep for all that time and wake up just in time to dress and sit
by the fire,—waiting for you to come in on March 18, I dont
think Id come to meet you darlint it always seems so ordinary
and casual for me to see you after such a long time—in the
street, I shall always want you to come straight to our home
and take me in both your arms and hold me for hours—and
you can't do that in the street or a station can you darlint. . . .
Darlint, pleased, happy, hopeful and yet sorry—that's how I
feel, can you understand? Sorry that Ive got to remain inactive
for more than another whole month, and I had thought by that
time I should be seeing you just as long and every time you
wanted me. However, for that glorious state of existence I
suppose we must wait for another three or four months.
Darlint, I am glad you succeeded Oh so glad I cant explain,
when your note came I didn't know how to work at all—all I
kept thinking of was your success—and my ultimate success I
hope.
I suppose it isnt possible for you to send it to me—not at all
possible, I do so chafe at wasting time darlint. He had a cold last
week and didnt go in, but came up to meet me about 5. Of
course I didnt know he was coming and it was funny—our
Monkey was on my desk—which must have been and Im
confident was noticed. [A toy monkey, a present from
Bywaters.]
Miss Prior told him we had not worked after 5 since last year
and he mentioned this to me—as much as to say 'How do you
account for saying you worked late some weeks ago' I didnt
offer any explanations. . . .
He also said 'Have you anything whatever belonging to him—
anything mind you' (I knew he meant our monkey) 'I have
nothing whatever belonging to him' I said—darlint it wasn't a
lie was it, because the monkey belongs to us doesn't it and not
to you or to me, and if it was a lie I dont care, I'd tell heaps

and heaps and heaps to help you even tho I know you don't
like them.

Darlint that reminds me you said in one of your letters 'It was
a lie and Peidi I hate them', about something I had or had not
told you and I forget which, but I am sure I told it to help us
both.

That hurt ever such a lot when I read it darlint, it hurts so
much that I couldn't talk to you about it at the time.

Darlint, do you think I like telling them, do you think I don't
hate it, darlint I do hate this life I lead—hate the lies hate
everything and I tell so many thats what hurts—it hits home
so hard—if only I could make an absolutely clean—fresh start
—it would all be so different—Id be so different too darlint
and we're going to start a new fresh clean life together soon
darlint, arent we tell me we are, tell me you are confident—
positive we are, I want telling all the time—to make me hope on.

Darlingest boy, this thing that I am going to do for both of us
will it ever—at all, make any difference between us, darlint, do
you understand what I mean. Will you ever think any the less
of me—not now, I know darlint—but later on—perhaps some
years hence—do you think you will feel any different—because
of this thing that I shall do.

Darlint—if I thought you would Id not do it, no not even so
that we could be happy for one day even one hour, Im not
hesitating darlint—through fear of any consequences of the
action, dont think that but I'd sooner go on in the old way for
years and years and years and retain your love and respect. I
would like you to write to me darlint and talk to me about this.

31 March 1922:
Darlingest Boy, This will be the last letter to England—I do
wish it wasn't, I wish you were never going away any more,
never going to leave me—I want you always to be with me. . . .
Pride of possession is a nice feeling don't you think darlint—
when it exists between you and me. . . .
*After tonight I am going to die . . . not really . . . but put on the
mask again darlint until the 26th May—doesn't it seem years and
years away? It does to me and I'll hope and hope all the time that
I'll never have to wear the mask any more after this time. Will
you hope and wish and wish too darlint . . . pour moi.
This time really will be the last you will go away . . . like things*

are, won't it? We said it before darlint I know and we failed . . .
but there will be no failure this next time darlint, there mustn't
be . . . I'm telling you . . . if things are the same again then I'm
going with you . . . wherever it is . . . if its to sea . . . I'm coming
too and if its to nowhere—I'm also coming darlint. You'll never
leave me behind again, never, unless things are different.

1 April 1922:
I saw Molly this morning. . . . What is she doing to herself?
She looked awfull—her face and lips are rouged terribly and
thick black lines pencilled under her eyes—and her face is
terribly thin fallen in under the cheek bones. Perhaps its
working in the West End. . . .
About that Thursday. . . . You say you're sorry for some
things that happened. Yes! I suppose I am in a way but
darlint, I feel I don't do enough. I want to show you how
large my love is and when it is something you want and you do
want it just at that moment don't you—I want to give it to
you—I want to stiffle all my own feelings for you. . . .
Darlint. I feel that I never want to withhold anything from
you—if you really want it and one of these days youre going to
teach me to give all and everything quite voluntarily—arent
you? Please darlint. . . .
Dont keep this piece.
About the Marconigram—do you mean one saying Yes or No,
because I shant send it darlint I'm not going to try any more
until you come back.
I made up my mind about this last Thursday.
He was telling his Mother etc. the circumstances of my 'Sunday
morning escapade' and he puts great stress on the fact of the tea
tasting bitter 'as if something had been put in it' he says. Now I
think whatever else I try it in again will still taste bitter—he will
recognise it and be more suspicious still and if the quantity is still
not successful—it will injure any chance I may have of trying
when you come home. . . .
I wish we had not got electric light—it would be easy.
I'm going to try the glass again occasionally—when it is safe.
I've got an electric light globe this time.

24 April 1922:
I used the 'light bulb' three times but the third time—he found a

piece—so I've given it up—until you come home. . . .
Why that passage in your last letter. The last time we met we
were pals, weren't we Chere?, why the question darlint if you
had wanted to write it, you should have stated it as a fact.
Of course we were pals, we always are and always will be,
while this life lasts—whatever else happens and alters our
lives—for better or for worse—for either or for both of us we
shall always remain that darlint—don't ask me the question
again—it hurts.

1 May 1922:
Darling isn't this a mistake 'Je suis gache, ma pauvre petite
amie'. This is how you wrote it.
I was glad you think and feel the same way as I do about the
'New Forest' [possibly the title of a novel]. *I don't think we're
failures in other things and we mustn't be in this. We mustn't give
up as we said. No, we shall have to wait if we fail again. Darlint,
Fate can't always turn against us and if it is we must fight
it—You and I are strong now We must be stronger. We must
learn to be patient.* We must have each other darlint. Its meant
to be I know I feel it is because I love you such a lot—such a
love was not meant to be in vain. It will come right I know one
day, if not by our efforts some other way. We'll wait eh
darlint, and you'll try and get some money and then we can go
away and not worry about anybody or anything. *You said it
was enough for an elephant. Perhaps it was. But you don't allow
for the taste making only a small quantity to be taken. It sounded
like a reproach was it meant to be?*
*Darlint I tried hard—you won't know how hard—because you
weren't there to see and I can't tell you all—but I did—I do want
you to believe I did for both of us.* . . .
The mail was in this morning and I read your letter darlint, I
cried—I couldn't help it—such a lot it sounded so sad I cried
for you I could exactly feel how you were feeling—I've felt
like that so often and I know.
*I was buoyed up with the hope of the 'light bulb' and I used a
lot—big pieces too—not powdered—and it has no effect—I quite
expected to be able to send that cable—but no—nothing has
happened from it and now your letter tells me about the bitter
taste again. Oh darlint, I do feel so down and unhappy.
Wouldn't the stuff make small pills coated together with soap and*

*dipped in liquorice powder—like Beechams—try while you're
away. Our Boy* [probably the messenger boy at her office] *had
to have his thumb operated on because he had a piece of glass in it
that's what made me try that method again—but I suppose as you
say he is not normal, I know I feel I shall never get him to take a
sufficient quantity of anything bitter. No I haven't forgotten the
key I told you before* [a reference to the Marconigram message
—'Yes' or 'No'—mentioned in her letter of 1 April 1922?].
Darlint two heads are better than one is such a true saying. You
tell me not to leave finger marks on the box—do you know I did
not think of the box but I did think of the glass or cup whatever was used. I wish I wish oh I wish I could do something.
Darlint, think for me, do. I do want to help. If you only knew
how helpless and selfish I feel letting you do such a lot for me
and I doing nothing for you. *If ever we are lucky enough to be
happy darling I'll love you such a lot. I always show you how
much I love you for all you do for me.* Its a terrible feeling
darlint to want—really want to give all and everything, and not
be able to give a tiny little thing—just thro' circumstances.
You asked me if Deborah described her feelings rightly when
she was talking about Kullett making love to her [in a novel
they had both read].
Darlingest boy, I don't think all the feelings can be put on
paper because there are not words to describe them. . . .
That month [Bywaters' next period of leave]—I can't bear to
think of it a whole four weeks and things the same as they are
now. All those days to live thro for just one hour in each.
*All that lying and scheming and subterfuge to obtain one little
hour in each day—when by right of nature and our love we
should be together for all the 24 in every day.*
Darlint don't let it be—I can't bear it all this time—the pain
gets too heavy to bear—heavier each day—but if things were
different what a grand life we should start together. . . .

18 May 1922:
'*It must be remembered that digitalin is a cumulative poison, and
that the same dose harmless if taken once, yet frequently repeated,
becomes deadly.*'
*Darlingest Boy,
The above passage I've just come across in a book I am reading
called 'Bella Donna' by Robert Hichens. Is it any use.* . . . .

13 June 1922:
Darlingest Boy,
I'm trying very hard—very very hard to B.B. ['be brave'] *I know my pal wants me to.*
On Thursday—he was on the ottoman at the foot of the bed and said he was dying and wanted to—he had another heart attack—thro me.
Darlint I had to laugh at this because I knew [these two words underlined] *it couldn't be a heart attack.*
When he saw this had no effect on me—he got up and stormed—I said exactly what you told me to and he replied that he knew thats what I wanted and he wasnt going to give it to me—it would make things far too easy for both of you (meaning you and me) especially for you he said. . . . .
I rang Avis yesterday and she said he came down there in a rage and told Dad everything. . . . Dad said it was a disgraceful thing that you should come between husband and wife and I ought to be ashamed. Darlint I told you this is how they would look at it—they dont understand and they never will any of them. . . .
Dad said to them 'What a scandal if it should get in the papers'. . . .

4 July 1922:
In one part of [your letter] you say you are going to still write to me because it will help, in another part you say—'Perhaps I shant write to you from some ports—because I want to help you.' I dont understand—I try to—but I cant—really I cant darlint—my head aches—aches with thinking sometimes.
Last Friday last year—we went to see 'Romance'—then we were pals and this year we seem no further advanced.
Why arnt you sending me something—I wanted you to—you never do what I ask you darlint—you still have your own way always—If I don't mind the risk why should you? whatever happens cant be any more than this existence—looking forward to nothing and gaining only ashes and dust and bitterness. . . .
Will you tell me if youd rather I didnt write?
                                        Peidi
Have you studied 'Bichloride of Mercury'?

19 September 1922:
Darlingest boy—I don't quite understand you about 'Pals'. You

say 'Can we be Pals only, Peidi, it will make it easier'.
Do you mean for always? because if you do, No, no, a thousand
times. We can't be 'pals' only [this word underlined] *for always*
darlint—its impossible physically and mentally.

Last time we had a long talk—I said, 'Go away this time and
forget all about me, forget you ever knew me, it will be
easier—and better for you.'

Do you remember—and you refused, so now I'm refusing
darlint—*it must be still 'the hope of all' or 'the finish of all'.*
If you still only mean for a certain time and you think it best,
*darlint it shall be so—I don't see how it will be easier myself—*but
it shall be as you say and wish, we won't be our natural selves
tho' I know—we'll be putting a kerb on ourselves the whole
time—like an iron bar that won't expand. Please don't let what
I have written deter you from any decision darlint—I don't
want to do that—truly I'd like to do what you think best. . . .
You sound very despondent when you say about 'Time passes and
with it some of the pain—Fate ordained our lot to be hard'. Does
some of the pain you [this word underlined] *feel pass with time?*
Perhaps it does—things seem so much easier to forget with a
man—his environment is always different—but with a woman its
always the same.
Darlint my pain gets less and less bearable—it hurts more and
more every day, every hour really.
'Other things only involve the parting of you and I, Peidi,
nobody deserves anything more than I do.'
I don't understand this part—try and explain to me please—
have you lost heart and given up hope? tell me if you have
darlint—don't bear it all alone. . . .
Now I'm going to be cross—Dont bully me [these three words
underlined]—I never said or even suggested that I should
cultivate the Regent Palace Hotel and there was no need
whatever for you to have hurled forth that edict and then
underlined it. Ask to be forgiven—you bully! (darlint pal). . . .
No, I dont think the man who mistook me for 'Romance' was
decent darlint, but I do think he was quite genuine in mistaking
me, I don't think it was a ruse on his part.
Yes, darlint you are jealous of him [this word underlined]*—but I*
want you to be—he has the right by law to all that you have the
right to by nature and love—yes darlint be jealous, so much so
that you will do something desperate. . . .

150

Before I finish up this letter Ive got a confession to make.
Darlingest about the watch—I didnt send it to Plymouth—
purposely.
I felt that you were not going to come and see me this time
and the feeling was awful—horrid, and I felt that if you
refused I couldnt make you.
And then I was tempted—I thought, 'Yes, I can make him—I
wont send his watch—I'll tell him if he wants it—he's to come
and fetch it.
Darlint, was it small? if it was, real big love must make people
think of small things, because real, big love made

Peidi

The last letter. 2 October 1922:
Darlingest lover of mine, thank you, thank you, oh thank you a
thousand times for Friday—it was lovely—its always lovely to go
out with you.
*And then Saturday—yes I did feel happy—*I didn't think a
teeny bit about anything in this world, except being with
you—and *all Saturday evening I was thinking about you*—I was
just with you in a big arm chair in front of a great big fire
feeling all the time how much I had won—cos I have darlint,
won such a lot—it feels such a great big thing to me
sometimes—that I can't breathe.
When you are away and I see girls with men walking along
together—perhaps they are acknowledged sweethearts—they
look so ordinary then I feel proud—so proud to think and feel
that you are my lover and even tho' not acknowledged I can
still hold you—just with a tiny 'hope'.
Darlint, we've said we'll always be Pals haven't we, shall we
say we'll always be lovers—even tho' secret ones, or is it (this
great big love) a thing we can't control—dare we say that—I
think I will dare. Yes I will 'I'll always love you'—if you are
dead—if you have left me even if you don't still love me, I
always shall you.
Your love to me is new, it is something different, it is my life
and if things should go badly with us, I shall always have this
past year to look back upon and feel that 'Then I lived' I
never did before and I never shall again.
Darlingest lover, what happened last night? I don't know
myself I only know how I felt—no not really how I felt but

how I could feel—if time and circumstances were different. It seems like a great welling up of love—of feeling—of inertia, just as if I am wax in your hands—to do with as you will and I feel that if you do as you wish I shall be happy, its physical purely and I can't really describe it—but you will understand darlint wont you? You said you knew it would be like this one day—if it hadn't would you have been disappointed. Darlingest when you are rough, I go dead—try not to be please. . . .

I tried so hard to find a way out of tonight darlingest but he was suspicious and still is—I suppose we must make a study of this deceit for some time longer. I hate it. I hate every lie I have to tell to see you—because lies seem such small mean things to attain such an object as ours. We ought to be able to use great big things for great big love like ours. I'd love to be able to say 'I'm going to see my lover tonight.' If I did he would prevent me—there would be scenes and he would come to 168 [168 Aldersgate Street, where she worked] and interfere and I couldn't bear that—I could be beaten all over at home and still be defiant—but at 168 it's different. It's my living—you wouldn't let me live on him would you and I shouldn't want to—darlint its funds that are our stumbling block—until we have those we can do nothing. Darlingest find me a job abroad. I'll go tomorrow and not say I was going to a soul and not have one little regret. I said I wouldn't think—that I'd try to forget—circumstances—Pal, help me to forget again—I have succeeded up to now—but its thinking of tonight and tomorrow when I can't see you and feel you holding me. Darlint—do something tomorrow night will you? something to make you forget. I'll be hurt I know, but I want you to hurt me—I do really—the bargain now seems so one sided—so unfair—but how can I alter it? . . .

Don't forget what we talked in the Tea Room, I'll still risk and try if you will—we only have 3¾ years left darlingest [they had made a pact to wait five years from 27 June 1921, Bywaters' nineteenth birthday and the day they thought of as the start of their love affair—'our first real birthday', as she called it]. Try & help

Peidi

⊙⊙⊙⊙⊙

While she was in prison awaiting trial, Edith Thompson was asked by her mother: 'How could you write those letters?'

'Nobody knows what kind of letters he was writing to me,' she replied.

The police traced only three letters from Frederick Bywaters to Mrs Thompson; the rest she had destroyed. Of these remaining letters, one had been written in December 1921 and was in the form of a Christmas greeting; cordial rather than romantic, it was signed 'Yours very Sincerely, Freddy' and was no doubt intended to be shown to Percy Thompson in a rather naive attempt to allay his suspicions. The style of the other letters, neither of which was dated, strikingly mirrored that of Mrs Thompson's; her often repeated claim that, in terms of compatibility, she and Bywaters were 'two halves' may have been an obvious and worn metaphor, but as far as their letter-writing was concerned, it was almost literally true. The shorter of the two letters read:

Darling Peidi Mia,
Tonight was impulse—natural—I couldn't resist—I had to hold you darling little sweetheart of mine—darlint I was afraid—I thought you were going to refuse to kiss me—darlint little girl—I love you so much and the only way I can control myself is by not seeing you and I'm not going to do that. Darlint Peidi Mia—I must have you—I love you darlint—logic and what others call reason do not enter into our lives, and where two halves are concerned. I had no intention darlint of doing that—it just happened thats all—I'm glad now chere—darlint when you suggested the occupied carriage, I didn't want to go in it—did you think that perhaps I did—so that there would have been no opportunity for me, to break the conditions that I had stipulated—darlint I felt quite confident that I would be able to keep my feelings down—I was wrong Peidi. I was reckoning on will power over ordinary forces—but I was fighting what? not ordinary forces—nothing was fighting the whole of me. Peidi you are my magnet—I cannot resist darlint—you draw me to you now and always, I shall never be able to see you and remain impassive. Darlint Peidi Mia Idol mine—I love you—always—always Ma Chere. Last night

L   153

when I read your questions I didn't know how to answer
them—I have now Peidi?
Darlint I dont think I can talk about other things tonight—I
want to hold you so tightly. I'm going to tonight in my sleep.
Bon Nuit Ma Petite, cherchez bien pour votre.

Freddy

✪✪✪✪✪

On 11 December 1922, after a five-day trial before Mr Justice
Shearman at the Old Bailey, both defendants were found guilty
of murder, and both were sentenced to death.

'I am not guilty,' Edith Thompson screamed. 'Oh God, I am
not guilty!' She was carried from the dock in a state of collapse.

Four days before Christmas the appeals were dismissed. Now,
unless the Home Secretary recommended a reprieve, Edith
Thompson would be the first woman executed since 1907, when
Mrs Rhoda Willis, a baby farmer, was hanged at Cardiff. The
division of public opinion as to whether or not the sentences
should be carried out on either or both of the prisoners was
represented microcosmically in the correspondence columns of
The Times. On the first day of the new year H. W. Massingham,
ex-editor of the *Star* and the *Daily Chronicle*, wrote:

Sir,
Will you allow me to summarise the case for commuting the
capital sentence on the Ilford prisoners?

FOR NOT HANGING MRS THOMPSON

1. That for the best part of a generation no woman in this
country has been hanged.
2. That within the knowledge of a leading counsel in the case, no
one in this country has been hanged in recent years unless he had
committed some physical act leading to murder.
3. That the Crown, in effect, rested their case on an attempt to
prove conspiracy to murder, and that this attempt failed.
4. That this line of argument rested largely on the production of
Mrs Thompson's letters, that if these documents showed any-

thing definite, it was a conspiracy to poison, and that the efforts of the Crown to prove such a conspiracy broke down.

5. That Mrs Thompson's conduct when the fatal assault took place went to show that she was genuinely horrified at it.

FOR NOT HANGING BYWATERS

1. That when this affection began he was a mere boy (he is still under 21), and that he bore a good character in his work and in his family relationships.

2. That his conduct in retaining Mrs Thompson's letters, though he had ample time to destroy them, was evidence that he did not regard them as compromising.

3. That in fact there is not the slightest evidence of his taking part in any conspiracy to poison.

4. That the assault on Mr Thompson, though savage, was committed in an open roadway in circumstances precluding the hope of escape or of any after life with Mrs Thompson.

5. That there was no evidence of his having bought a knife for the purpose of the crime, and that, therefore, presumably he carried it with him, as seafaring men not infrequently do.

AGAINST HANGING EITHER OF THEM

That in trying the two cases together, and in insisting on the final right to reply, the Crown increased the chances of a verdict against both prisoners; and that the Home Office, in considering, as it is entitled to do, these circumstances, as well as the whole psychology of the letters, has vested in it both a right and a duty to mitigate the extreme sentence of the law.

The following day, Hugh J. Goolden put the opposing viewpoint:

FOR HANGING MRS THOMPSON

1. A woman was hanged in 1907. Since then the law has never been altered to provide any substitution in the penalty for murder by a woman.

2. I do not understand the expression 'some physical act leading to murder'. I imagine that anything short of mere negligence, on

the part of one of the accused, to prevent the commission of the crime is sufficiently a 'physical act' when two persons are indicted for murder. Both the Eastbourne murderers [Field and Gray] were hanged.

3. The Crown indicted the prisoners for wilful murder. I understand that the count relating to conspiracy was not proceeded with. The prisoners were tried as principals in the first and second degree respectively.

4. The letters showed not a *conspiracy*, but an *incitement*, to poison. The fact that Thompson happened to be stabbed and not poisoned is no defence.

5. Mrs Thompson was 'genuinely horrified'. A natural climax after months of plotting.

FOR HANGING BYWATERS

1. The 'mere boy' of this type knows a great deal more about the world than the public-school boy of the same age. His 'business' character and his 'domestic' character may not agree with each other.

2. It is notorious that love-letters are more often kept than destroyed, however incriminating.

3. See my answer No. 4, above.

4. The assault itself was a desperate one, committed by a desperate, unthinking man.

5. I cannot believe that the stewards of the P. & O. walk about with large knives in their overcoats. This man is not the type of 'seafaring man' suggested by Mr Massingham's argument.

IN FAVOUR OF HANGING BOTH OF THEM

The Court of Criminal Appeal decided that Mr Justice Shearman was perfectly right in declining to try the two cases separately. It was pointed out that, had the trials been separate ones, the verdict would have been substantially the same.

The penalty for murder is one of those penalties which happen to be fixed by law. That penalty is death.

A letter from Sir Herbert Stephen, Clerk of Assize for the Northern Circuit, appeared on 4 January:

Sir,

I feel justified in offering to your readers, with your permission, a few words about Mr Massingham's summary of the 'case for commuting the capital sentence', because I am entirely confident that the Secretary of State, whose duty it is to be thoroughly and accurately acquainted with the facts and the law, will be in no way and in no degree influenced in his conduct by the opinions of imperfectly informed outsiders like Mr Massingham and myself. In the first place, I assume, as the public ought to assume, that the jury delivered the right verdict, and the Court of Criminal Appeal the right judgement. This assumption disposes of about half of Mr Massingham's arguments. It is beside the point to say that there was 'no evidence' of this or that detail. All that, with the assistance of the best efforts of counsel on both sides, has been decided by the verdict of the jury, and the decision has been confirmed on appeal as lawful and regular.

The first reason stated by Mr Massingham 'for not hanging Mrs Thompson' is that no woman has been hanged in this country for a good many years. The argument is that of an old-fashioned and rather timid Conservative. Two years ago the Legislature, by an Act of the widest application, removed, as thoroughly as legislation could remove, all the disadvantages, or supposed disadvantages, which women suffered merely by reason of their sex. It must have intended also to remove—again as far as possible— the 'sex disqualifications' which tended in the other direction. If there was some plausibility before 1920 in the proposition that a woman's sex disqualified her from suffering capital punishment, there is none now.

The next reason is somewhat metaphysical—that no one has recently been hanged 'unless he had committed some physical act leading to murder'. It is a physical act to speak, and a physical act to write, and the verdict establishes—conclusively, as far as the public is concerned—that by speech or writing, if by no other physical acts, Mrs Thompson did something 'leading to murder'. All Mr Massingham's reasons 'for not hanging Bywaters' are in reality topics suitable to be urged for the defence before the jury, and were no doubt most ably urged by the proper people at the proper time.

Mr Massingham's last reason for commutation of the sentences is that the Crown, by trying the two cases together and insisting on the right of reply, 'increased the chances of a verdict against both prisoners'. When a crime has been committed, and persons alleged to be guilty of it are prosecuted, it is the duty of the Crown to 'increase the chance' of conviction by every legitimate means, just as much as it is to allow every opportunity to the defence for increasing the chances of acquittal. If the Crown might not increase the chance of conviction, they would never be able to offer any material evidence, and there would be no criminal trials.

⊕⊖⊕⊖⊕

The sentences were carried out simultaneously on the morning of 9 January 1923. Frederick Bywaters, who was hanged at Pentonville, is said to have gone to his death with firmness and assurance, while Edith Thompson, whose hair had turned grey since the trial, had to be carried, half-conscious, to the gallows at Holloway.

For many years afterwards, discussion of the case was impeded by emotion; but distance lends the mind impartiality, and now, nearly half a century later, one can look at the facts dispassionately and say that Edith Thompson was certainly guilty on at least *some* counts—adding, with the smugness of hindsight, that whatever her crimes, the penalty of death was disgustingly inappropriate, far more immoral than all her transgressions.

The irony of her fate is that if she, rather than her lover, had killed Percy Thompson, she would probably have been reprieved. There were 832,104 signatories to a petition for the reprieve of Bywaters: far greater support than was received for a similar petition on her behalf. The Home Secretary—humane but human, a politician, a member of a party that would continue to govern only if public opinion decreed—must have been influenced by the imbalance between the number of signatures on the two petitions. To have reprieved one prisoner but not the other would have caused a storm of outrage, and there were insufficient grounds for interfering with the sentence on Bywaters.

Fifty-four women found guilty of murder had escaped a

gallows death since 1907. Edith Thompson would have stood an
excellent chance of joining that number had she succeeded in
poisoning her husband.

Bibliography

Much of the information contained in this book was culled from newspaper reports. Among the books and journal articles consulted, the following were particularly valuable.

1 Correspondence Course
Duke, Winifred. *The Stroke of Murder* (1937)
Walsh, Sir Cecil. *The Agra Double Murder* (1929)

2 Irene Munro
Adamson, Iain. *A Man of Quality: A Biography of Mr Justice Cassels* (1964)
Bowker, A. E. *Behind the Bar* (1948)
Browne, Douglas G., and Tullett, E. V. *Bernard Spilsbury: His Life and Cases* (1951)
Duke, Winifred (see 1 above)
Duke, Winifred (Ed). *Trial of Field and Gray* (1935)
Knowles, Leonard. *Court of Drama: Famous Trials at Lewes Assizes* (1966)
Marjoribanks, Edward. *The Life of Sir Edward Marshall Hall* (1929)
Wild, Roland, and Curtis-Bennett, Derek. *'Curtis': The Life of Sir Henry Curtis-Bennett, KC* (1937)

3 Lonely Hearts
Brown, Wenzell. *The Lonely Hearts Killers* (originally *Introduction to Murder*) (New York 1965)
Hoffmann, Dr Richard H. 'The Untold Story of Martha', *True Crime Detective* (USA, Fall 1951)

4   Young England
Benson, Captain L. *The Book of Remarkable Trials and Notorious Characters from 'Half-Hanged Smith', 1700, to Oxford who Shot at the Queen, 1840* (1871)

6   Rising Sun
Hogarth, Basil (Ed). *Trial of Robert Wood* (1936)
Lustgarten, Edgar. *Defender's Triumph* (1951)
Marjoribanks, Edward (see 2 above)

7   Sacco–Vanzetti
Ehrmann, Herbert B. *The Case That Will Not Die: Commonwealth vs. Sacco and Vanzetti* (1970)
Fraenkel, Osmund K. *The Sacco–Vanzetti Case* (1931)
Frankfurter, Marion D., and Jackson, Gardner. *The Letters of Sacco and Vanzetti* (1928)
Musmanno, Michael A. *Verdict!* (1958)
Russell, Francis. *Tragedy in Dedham: The Story of the Sacco-Vanzetti Case* (1963)

8   Red Barn
Anonymous. *An Authentic History of Maria Marten; or, The Red Barn! with A Full Account of the Discovery of the Murder through Dreams; Inquest on the Body; Apprehension, Trial, Remarkable Defence, Committal, Conviction, Execution, and Dissection of the Body of the Prisoner; to which is added Fifty-three Letters, in Answer to his Advertisement for a Wife!!* (London, nd)
Curtis, J. *The Murder of Maria Marten* (1928)
Foster, William. *Advertisement for Wives* (1828)
Gibbs, Dorothy, and Maltby, Herbert. *The True Story of Maria Marten* (1949)
McCormick, Donald. *The Red Barn Mystery* (1967)

9   Spelling Mistakes
Cherrill, Fred. *Cherrill of the Yard* (1954)
Wensley, Frederick P. *Detective Days: The Record of Forty-two Years' Service in the Criminal Investigation Department* (1930)

Woodland, W. Lloyd (Ed). *The Trial of Thomas Henry Allaway* (1929)

10 Starr Faithfull
Cook, Fred J. *The Girl on the Lonely Beach* (New York 1956)
Markey, Morris. 'The Mysterious Death of Starr Faithfull', included in *The Aspirin Age*, Isabel Leighton (Ed) (1950)
O'Hara, John. *Butterfield 8* (fiction) (1969)
Packer, Peter. *The Love Thieves* (fiction) (1963)

11 Newgate Finale
Felstead, S. T., and Muir, Lady. *Sir Richard Muir: The Memoirs of a Public Prosecutor* (1927)

12 Edith Thompson
Bresler, Fenton. *Reprieve: A Study of a System* (1965)
Broad, Lewis. *The Innocence of Edith Thompson* (1952)
Wild, Roland, and Curtis-Bennett, Derek (see 2 above)
Young, Filson (Ed). *Trial of Frederick Bywaters and Edith Thompson* (1923)

Index